Learning through Fun & Games

ELYSSEBETH LEIGH

JEFF KINDER

**40 GAMES AND SIMULATIONS
FOR TRAINERS, FACILITATORS
AND MANAGERS**

The McGraw-Hill Companies, Inc.

Sydney New York San Francisco Auckland
Bangkok Bogotá Caracas Hong Kong
Kuala Lumpur Lisbon London Madrid
Mexico City Milan New Delhi San Juan
Seoul Singapore Taipei Toronto

McGraw·Hill Australia

A Division of The **McGraw·Hill** Companies

National Library of Australia Cataloguing-in-Publication data:

Leigh, Elyssebeth.
Serious learning through fun and games.

ISBN 0 07 470768 X.

1. Educational games – Australia. 2. Adult education –
Australia. 3. Simulation games in education – Australia.
I. Title.

374.22

Published in Australia by
McGraw-Hill Book Company Australia Pty Limited
4 Barcoo Street, Roseville NSW 2069, Australia
Acquisitions Editor: Kristen Baragwanath
Production Editor: Sybil Kesteven
Editor: Sarah Baker
Designer: R.T.J. Klinkhamer
Illustrator: Lorenzo Lucia
Cartoonist: Fiona Katauskas
Typeset in 12/15 Bembo by R.T.J. Klinkhamer
Printed on 80 gsm woodfree by Best Tri Colour Printing & Packaging Co. Ltd,
Hong Kong.

Contents

About the authors

Elyssebeth Leigh graduated from Sydney University with a BA DipEd and an ambition to teach teenagers, when she was just 20 years old. Early experiences in high schools confirmed that Elyssebeth's unconventional approach to teaching challenges the status quo. This did not stop her working—and time spent with pre-school and primary classes, aboriginal students, police recruits, and women with ambitions to return to work taught her a great deal about how to work with learners according to their age and needs.

For the past ten years she has taught adults at the University of Technology, Sydney in the Faculty of Education while continuing her own study, gaining two postgraduate degrees. She has plans to complete her doctoral thesis in 2000.

She has worked on the NSW committees of two professional organisations (the Australian Institute of Training and Development (AITD) and the Australian Human Resources Institute (AHRI)) and is a member of the International Simulation and Gaming Association (ISAGA) international committee.

Elyssebeth and her husband celebrated 30 years of marriage in 1999. They have two sons.

For Mick, Michael and Glenn who supported (and survived) my early forays into the fascinating world of learning through playing. My thanks and love always.

Jeff Kinder, BEd (Adult Education), says that life is a game of adapting and flexing. He started his career skating in the big ice shows of Europe and America. To rise above the competition, he skated on stilts and for this he won a World Record (still unchallenged today), but the game of life plays on. In his mid-30s, Jeff went back to school to gain a degree in Adult Education majoring in human resource development. It was during this time that he met Elyssebeth and developed Strategic Learning Solutions, which links games and simulations with 'bottom line' business solutions, providing effective training and learning that's fun!

For Clare Whyte, who never stopped learning.

Acknowledgments

Thanks to Maree Hill and Simona Williamson for vital help with administration of the project and layout; also thanks to Bryan Turner for reading some of the drafts.

Compiling the introduction was a team effort. Special thanks are due to Gwen Daly, Gillian Seils and Jeff Weil.

Congratulations to these designers:

Alison Henderson and Brian Hennessy: How to hit a moving hedgehog
Lana Kuczynski: World peace
Jeff Kinder: Learning to learn (LTL), Personal learning outcomes—tropical style!, Territorial terrain, Stand on the line—scattergram
Fiona Loschiavo: Boarding pass to the New World
Steve Renwick: Trust me
Michael Broad: Team resources
Andrew Boulton: Problems up and down
John Merino: Consensiball
Sandra Sheehan: Circle of safety
Kelly Scott: Bridging the gap
Janell Carter: Chaordic construction
Joanna Halioris: Playground
Elyssebeth Leigh and Don Chantler: RiftRaft Inc.
Pia Christensen: Mars huts
Lyn Alderman: Any noise annoys an oyster
Dianne King: 'What would you know?'
Sally Jeffry: How to be an egg-spert!
Yolanda de Winter: Whose rules are these anyway?
Richard Sebel: Where is it?
Carmen Richardson and Wayne Townson: Get it? Do it!
Maree Jaloussis: Recapping review
Maria Dimolianis and Sally Frielander Gordon: Rallycross
Michael Sara: Learning organisation
Maree Argy: What is it?
Ruth Hanbury: The essence
Richard George East: Retail ordering and stock control
Barbara Dobosz: Irish preferences
Gary Seaton: Approaching safety
Peter Bainbridge: What *bugs* you about a meeting?
Gillian Seils: Coloured names

Ray Mortlock: Say hullo
Suzanne Vucurovic: Famous faces
Sandra Wood: Getting to know you
Carol Shaw: Whom am I meeting?
Sandra Chung: Coloured shapes
Judith Williamson: CARP (clarify and reinforce points)
Elyssebeth Leigh: Exploring ethical dilemmas

Introduction

Welcome to a book of *simulations* and *games* for use by managers, learning co-ordinators, consultants, adult educators, teachers, trainers, facilitators and students. It contains a wide variety of activities for use in, or adaptation to suit, contemporary learning situations.

These activities can be an alternative to traditional teaching and can also support it. They can motivate and promote interest, and put fun into learning. They encourage skill development and help in the acquisition of critical thinking, information analysis, questioning skills, interpersonal communication, and problem identification and solving. They can provoke attitude change, and lead to greater understanding and participation in personal and organisational development. They provide opportunities for creating deeper self-awareness, interpersonal skills and leadership capabilities.

The activities were designed as assessment tasks during study for the Bachelor of Education in Adult Education at the University of Technology, Sydney (UTS). They have been trialled and evaluated as part of this process and rated as highly effective. Much of the work is original, while some is adapted from activities first developed in widely different contexts. They are a testimony to the varied backgrounds of the designers who drew on their experience in retail, health, manufacturing, finance and social services to create engaging and memorable learning events.

The designers are all working in the broad field of adult education—in all its complexity—and are acutely aware of the difficulty of ensuring that new learning has been absorbed, critically examined and integrated into understanding and behaviour. Most are, or have been, students or staff of the Faculty of Education at the University of Technology, Sydney (UTS).

When time is short, many experts simply tell their audiences 'the facts', relying on the listening skills of their audience to enable the transfer of knowledge. This reliance on 'telling' ignores the reality that many people do not find it easy to learn from hearing information, but prefer to learn through involvement and active engagement of all their senses.

The designers suggest that there is no need to rely solely on your expertise when using their activities—the participants will also teach, and learn from, each other.

SPECIAL CONSIDERATIONS

Whenever you choose to run an activity, it is important to take account of the probability that you have people with differing capabilities and limitations participating. Consider issues such as:

- Hearing impairment (or deafness): for example, some participants may rely on lip-reading, or experience hearing difficulties caused by background noise generated by enthusiastic players.
- Vision impairment (or blindness): for example, colour blindness may cause problems if you are using colour coding to guide action and decisions.
- Mobility impairment: wheelchair access, eye level contact and the degree of ability to move independently may all need to be considered in choosing activities.
- Level of prior learning: many of your participants may be bilingual and still in the process of perfecting their English language usage, numeracy and/or literacy skills.

Consider how to shape each activity to enable the participation of each person present. Ensure there are quiet times for those who need extra time to absorb the impact of the action, and use seating arrangements for small group work and large group discussions which allow lip-readers, and those less able to move around, to see everyone clearly.

Where a participant has a helper, assist them to keep up with the discussion and, where necessary, ensure that they have sufficient prior warning of what may happen, so that they can quickly and accurately communicate key messages between you, the player, the larger group, etc. A few minutes spent with such helpers—before the turbulence of the action—will provide a smoother transition to the action and mean that you are directly modelling a stance for equity of opportunity by your actions (which always speak louder than words). Try to ensure that helpers are effective in their support of the learning process and are not forced to interrupt you for additional information at inopportune moments, when you are least able to disrupt the process.

QUESTIONS TO GUIDE CHOICES

The basic philosophy of providing *learning through fun and games* also influences other forms of active learning, including adventure learning, outdoor learning and other forms of experiential learning. Like all powerful tools, these activities require a framework for making appropriate selections to suit particular learning contexts. To be successful requires a clear and focused concept of what you are seeking to achieve and must be linked to a planned approach to taking action. A vague idea that 'this activity could work' will not be sufficient.

We suggest that successful use of simulations and games requires thoughtful answers to these three questions:

1. Why do you want to present your material in this way?

There are many possible reasons for using a simulation or game to support the learning process. Some of these reasons may relate to your own preferences for working with learners. Others may concern the knowledge and capabilities which you want to help people acquire. Possible reasons for choosing an activity from this book include:

Benefits for individuals

- *Overcoming fear, coping with change and the unfamiliar:* Learners frequently describe how they overcame personal difficulties in pursuit of a goal by participating in an activity which helped them, in some very particular way, to analyse and understand their own circumstances. They gained a new understanding of themselves and were able to adjust behaviour and attitudes to meet changing life circumstances.
- *Trust:* Active engagement in the learning process can encourage people to more fully trust themselves and others.
- *Counteracting stress:* A break from familiar classroom routines can ease the stress of concerns about personal ability to memorise and recall information correctly.
- *Fun/excitement:* Learning while having fun makes the experience memorable and can generate enthusiasm—even in reluctant participants!
- *Health:* Active participation can stimulate physical and mental well-being. When learners have been passive for some time, movement and conversation can renew interest in the learning process.
- *Self-esteem:* Active involvement encourages self-respect and enhances feelings of self-worth and confidence.
- *Goal setting:* Active encounters with knowledge linked to personal goals can support reflective assessment of the effectiveness of goal-setting efforts.
- *Initiative and achievement:* Team members are often surprised that they have achieved more than they initially thought possible and gain external feedback on their real capabilities.
- *Responsibility:* Individuals experiencing the actual effects of their actions gain an increased awareness of responsibility.

Benefits for groups

- *Co-operation:* Many life and work tasks cannot be achieved without group co-operation—first-hand experience in a practice setting can help individuals to extend their group work skills.
- *Improving communication:* Representations of reality demand the same kind of effective interpersonal interactions and communication as is needed for the 'real thing'.
- *Risk taking:* Stepping out of comfort zones to attempt something new is a key factor in many of these activities. Sharing responsibility for failure and for success supports the willingness to take risks and achieve new skills.
- *Decision making:* Active learning involves participants in making individual and/or group decisions.
- *Problem solving:* Techniques for solving difficult situations can be trialled safely.
- *Personal accountability:* Learners see, hear and feel the effects of their decisions—on themselves and others.
- *Leadership:* A relatively risk-free arena for trying leadership techniques can be provided.
- *Negotiation techniques:* Learners practise negotiation skills and/or experience the results of others' attempts at negotiating.
- *Observation skills:* Learners may increase their awareness of ways that others make decisions, interact and affect the group. As well as more obvious physical observations, they may also learn to detect attitudinal changes in themselves and others.
- *Group dynamics/team building:* Team experience leads to a greater understanding of how groups work (or don't work) together.
- *Commitment building:* It is widely held that people are more committed to a decision when they've been part of the decision-making process. Using representational activities, such as the ones in this book, can demonstrate the truth of this assertion and help individuals gain insight into ways to appropriately influence others to commit to a goal.

2. What do you actually want to achieve?

Use a simulation or game when you want people to have an emotional and physical experience of *being involved in* an event, task or process. Simulations and games—such as the activities included in this book—focus on the learning process and action, as well as on the content. For example, there are many print sources of instructions and preparation for a job interview (even multiple-choice tests on being interviewed), but only the actual experience of being interviewed gives the mental and emotional seasoning that can make a difference when it comes to the 'real thing'.

When you want to achieve an 'embodied' understanding of new concepts, these designs provide a basis for structuring active learning to enable first-hand 'experience' in a safe environment. Specific changes to behaviour are best achieved when people have had a physical experience of what the new behaviour will 'feel' like. Like athletes, whose dedication to physical improvement 'records' new knowledge throughout their body, simulations and learning games provide the same kind of physical 'recording' or 'embodiment' of new knowledge. Ideas do not remain frozen as intellectual exercises; rather they become famil-iar routines easier to recall and act on, in the kinds of circumstances anticipated by the designers.

When you want your participants to under-stand their own level of responsibility, get them involved in the action. Watching while someone else tells them what to do is less effective than having to 'do it' themselves while knowing they will have to explore and explain 'why' they did 'what' they did.

3. How do you want to do it?
Why do you want to do it that way?

The next section of this introduction contains ideas to consider in developing your own answers to this question. In short, we suggest that you must be confident of your ability to manage the learning process. You must also be aware of the extent to which you will not be in charge of the action.

Beware: If you believe that, as the educator, you must control all the action, don't use these activities. They all assume that the facilitator of the process is able to stand aside from involvement in the action and thereby help partici-pants learn from their experiences and the results of their own actions.

HOW ARE GAMES LISTED IN THIS BOOK?

Familiarise yourself with the quick, look-up matrix on page 30. This special feature is a key to identifying games to suit possible learning goals. Each designer identified several possible learning outcomes for their activities. The editors categorised these outcomes into eight types and have designed the accompanying icons to help you identify suitable activities for your own learning goals. We do not intend these categories to be either exhaustive or definitive, and we encourage you not to be constrained by our ideas. They are guides and helpers, not straightjackets. Our eight categories are:

1. Trust, change and solving problems

2. Frame games

3. Specialist knowledge and using technology

4. Icebreakers

5. Revision of learning

6. Communication, conflict, negotiation and cultures

7. Planning and organising

8. Energisers

Each designer has provided detailed instructions for running their activity. Each one is suitable for several different categories, as indicated by the icons displayed at the top of the first page of each activity. This does not mean that any activity is exclusively or primarily suitable for only these categories. Every activity involves using information; most involve working in groups and/or teams, many require planning and organising, and so on. Your choices are really only limited by your own creativity. Allow enough time to be confident about your reasoning and then prepare carefully and thoughtfully and, remember, always be ready for the unexpected! Simulations and games come with the guarantee that the learning will be intense and memorable and seldom quite what you expected.

Ticks on the quick look-up matrix indicate the categories for which, we believe, each activity is readily suitable (see p. 30).

THE STRUCTURE AND KEY FEATURES OF SIMULATIONS AND GAMES

While all the activities in this book are superficially quite different, they share a number of common characteristics. This section describes what these are and why it is important that you know about them and understand their significance.

I. The sequence of events

Every activity has three stages through which it passes. These are usually known as the *briefing*, *action* and *debriefing* phases. It is essential to understand the characteristics of each stage and the different behaviours required of the educator in each one.

The briefing

The briefing is that important few minutes before the action begins. At this time you have to:

- introduce the activity;
- outline the learning goals it has been selected to address;
- explain why this activity has been chosen for inclusion in the context in which you are working;
- say what you expect might be gained from participation in the activity.

The one key rule for you to remember to apply during the briefing is this: *do not pre-empt the learning.*

This rule simply means that you must be able to describe the general characteristics of the activity, but *never* state conclusively what will be learnt as a result of taking part. This rule is very important. It prevents disappointment when participants actually do something radically different from what is expected, or do not do what you were expecting. It allows room for new and unexpected learning to occur, and be identified and understood by everyone. It protects you as well, since it helps prevent you from making predictions that may not come true on particular occasions. Remember also that it is important to avoid predicting something that then does not happen.

When you introduce any structured activity to a group of participants you cannot fully predict exactly what will happen next. It is a little like a roller-coaster ride. You know it will be noisy and fast and (perhaps) great fun, but you do not know exactly when it will hit the heights or begin its plunge down the next slope. So you hang on all the time and allow it to carry you along. When the ride is over everyone may want to say quite a lot about their feelings and the nature of the experience.

We provide the 'Do not…' version of this rule first because the positive version is a little more complicated. It goes like this: *briefly introduce the rules, describe the overall process (in very general terms, according to the designer's instructions) and remind everyone to be alert for other learning outcomes along the way.*

For example, there are a number of icebreakers included in this book. To introduce them you could say something like: 'We are going to spend a few minutes in an activity that can help us to learn more about each other. I will give you some instructions and then you have [the designated number of] minutes to complete the activity according to my instructions. Our main goal is to learn more about who we are, and to share something about ourselves with each other. We may learn more than we expect, so remember to stay alert to new ideas and facts.'

During the briefing phase allow time to ensure everyone knows what to do. Distribute any necessary materials. Answer general questions about the activity without giving away any details that might forewarn them about facts and ideas you want them to discover for themselves.

Where it is important that everyone hears the same thing, each of our authors has provided carefully worded instructions to read out to everyone. The *description* and *learning opportunity* sections of each game should *not* be read aloud.

During the briefing phase you are the centre of attention and have almost total power over the group. As you move on to the action, you are about to relinquish almost all of this!

The action

During this middle phase of any simulation or game activity, the facilitator is virtually redundant and must stay out of the way—except where specific directions by a designer require you to act in some particular manner to help move the action along. Participants' actions are the focus of attention in the debriefing phase so you don't want to have anyone saying: 'I only did [whatever is being commented on] because you told me to.' Such a response draws you into a process of justifying and explaining yourself at the very time when you most need to have the spotlight on participants' behaviour, not your own!

It is often a good idea to select a quiet corner before you even introduce the activity, and then retire to that spot as soon as the action begins. If possible, find a spot where you can see without intruding on anyone else's line of sight. In this way the action will unfold almost like a play before you. The events can then be explored in the third (debriefing) phase with your contributions being limited to comments on observed behaviour and questions to elicit reasons for particular actions.

If something seems to be going 'wrong' (for example, people appear lost or are not obeying the rules you have read out), you can stop the action, review the rules and then allow the action to proceed, or move straight into the debriefing. Your choice of action at this point will depend on your assessment of how much can be gained by taking either path. If a lot has happened and you think there is enough for participants to discuss, you may choose to end the activity at this point. On the other hand, it may be that you have had to re-state the rules almost at once: in this case re-read the rules and then again step away from the centre of attention.

The debriefing

This is the final phase and will involve some quiet time for private reflection as well as group discussion. A 'rule of thumb' for the debriefing is that it requires about as much time as the briefing and the action combined. It can be shorter, or much longer, depending on the particular activity you are using, and the amount of learning which participants draw from their own, and others', behaviour. A good process for helping everyone prepare for the discussion is as follows:

- Call 'Stop' loudly, then wait until everyone has stopped moving and talking (or use a bell, a musical cue or other form of familiar sound to attract everyone's attention).
- Allow full silence to settle over the group.
- Say 'Thank you', and then follow this with brief suggestions as to how everyone might arrange themselves to facilitate the discussion. A circle is often the best arrangement for ensuring that everyone is involved in the discussion, so you might ask everyone to bring a chair to a central spot in the room and form a circle. If you are working at a large central table you might ask everyone to draw up their chair and face the centre. Once everyone is seated, suggest that they sit quietly for a few moments to collect their thoughts and prepare for the discussion.

Reflective learners will appreciate this opportunity to draw together all their thoughtful observations, which might become lost if everyone is talking at once. Active learners—who may have been the people most involved in the process—may appreciate the time to come to grips with what they have been doing. And people who need a strong theoretical or practical framework with which to appreciate the value of learning from the experience may use this time to focus on questions they need answered.

One effective sequence of questions that is helpful in guiding discussion is the following:

Q1: What happened? Encourage everyone to describe the action from their own point of view and conversely encourage everyone else to listen carefully, to find similarities with their own experience, and to identify major differences. Both 'same' and 'different' experiences can help enlarge everyone's learning.

Q2: How do you feel? It is important to help people name their feelings, since unexpressed emotions (positive or negative) can influence human behaviour more than we usually realise. Don't take this as a suggestion to dwell on them or try to extract them if no one seems willing to speak. Remember that the participants may be learning to express how they are feeling as a result of being involved in any kind of learning activity and are gaining in their ability to understand how they respond to different things around them. People need time to become more sensitive to their world, so hasten slowly. Use silence to encourage people to offer their observations.

Silence is a powerful tool at this point. Everyone may appear to be waiting for you to speak, but if you maintain a friendly silence this can prompt others to 'fill the silence' and they will bring up things that are important to them and about which you are entirely unaware. It may be helpful for you to practise this 'stance of silence' in other settings. As you learn more about the feelings of anxiety which arise when a group is silent you will be able to manage your own anxiety and use your stillness to encourage others to speak.

Sometimes people mistake 'behaviour' words for 'feeling' words. If this seems to be happening in a group with which you are working, try the following strategy: silently identify whether each word being offered as a 'feeling' word is actually about feelings or behaviours/actions and, as you work with the group, write each new word in one of two sections on the board or flip chart. You will have decided (but not announced) which section of the board is for feelings and which is for behaviours. When it seems appropriate (e.g. there are enough words in each category), you can stand back from both lists and invite participants to comment on anything they observe about the lists. A process like this can help everyone understand more about what was happening during the action and encourage discussion about what happens in similar situations in real life.

It has been our observation that men are often less likely to make clear and powerful statements about feelings. You can sometimes feel like a dentist extracting teeth if you are attempting to encourage men to say how they are feeling. On one occasion an observant facilitator wrote on the whiteboard each 'feeling' word that was offered. After a few minutes speakers began to say things like: 'It's like that word on the board. I was "angry". They didn't listen to my suggestions and we were last to finish. I knew we could do better so I was "frustrated" too.' That list of words proved highly beneficial in encouraging others to attempt to identify how they were feeling.

Q3: What are some real-life parallels between what happened here, and the 'real world' represented by this activity? How can these parallels help you to learn more about [the topic]? The answers to these questions are probably the main reason you chose the activity. They are designed to help everyone focus their attention on the entire experience in order to identify what happened and how this does represent aspects of their own familiar lives. Thus an activity might encourage communication skills practice, yet some will not see it the way others do. This can be the cause of fruitful discussion about how to help others see your point of view, while you are learning to see theirs!

Some general comments about debriefing

There is usually not a great need for you to say much in the debriefing. Your role is to guide the conversation and to draw the quiet group members out by asking them for their answers to each of the three questions or for their observations about the events as they unfolded. Some facilitators like to use the debriefing to impart their opinions of what they saw happening. There are, however, distinct benefits in encouraging the participants to tell each other, and then to add your comments only where specific things that you saw occurring, and that have a potential to enhance the learning, have not been mentioned.

As noted above, silence is a very powerful tool during the debriefing. It can slow down the conversation so that everyone has a chance to make new mental connections and then offer them to the whole group. It can also help to slow down the talkative group members. You may like to try this kind of comment: 'Let's have no one speak for half a minute while we consider how this particular feature of the activity could be like real life.' During the next 30 seconds, sit quietly with your mouth firmly closed to encourage others to reflect on the question you have posed. Then invite comments and renew the discussion.

Another debriefing strategy that helps everyone in having their say is to have people work in pairs or trios to review all three questions and then return to the large group with their joint response. Then the members of the pairs or trios can summarise what they discussed as the most important aspects about the sequence of events, feelings and parallels with real life, etc.

2. The four key elements in all simulations and games

There are four key elements in any simulation. These four elements are:

- the scenario, within which the action occurs;
- the rules of play;
- the roles adopted by players;
- the recording system.

These elements are, of course, parts of a whole activity but players will require an understanding of what each one is, because discussion during the debriefing will refer to each one and its particular real-life parallel. Each one can be introduced separately during the briefing. Players are thus able to acquire enough information to get inside the action and yet, afterwards, be able to distinguish among the different facets of their experience.

The scenario

This is the term used to describe all that information which is provided to the players about the setting in which the action takes place. It may be given verbally, or in writing. For example, players may simply be told: 'You are members of the community called "Poortown" in which there are citizens, shopkeepers, police, clergy and social workers.' Alternatively, players may be given written material, including maps, weather forecasts, photos, political information, etc. The scenario might represent an aspect of a known situation (e.g. a disaster may approximate the scene after Cyclone Tracy hit Darwin in 1974). In many cases the scenario is simply an explanation of the setting in which the action which will be taking place.

Visual aids may be provided in the form of wall charts, name plates, or even particular settings of furniture, and so on. Whatever the means used, the aim is to help players invoke internally a 'sense of occasion' within which the action will take place. As far as possible the players are given a shared understanding on which to base later discussions. Rather than preventing the emergence of differences in perception, the use of a carefully constructed scenario often underlines the extremely varied ideas which, given the same basic information, people can develop.

The rules

The rules, in effect, shape the progress of the action. They describe what behaviour is permissible, and what is not. They are part of the initiating fabric of the game and help create the environment. Rules exist on two levels. The higher level of rules are those laid down by the game itself. Some facilitators use a 'Games Overall Director' (or G.O.D.) label to emphasise the power of these rules within the context of the game. Tidal movements, sunrise and wind direction are all real-world parallels of the G.O.D.'s rules. The second level of rules are the 'people' or 'mindset' rules, which people utilise to explain and/or manage the world around them, and apply to the experience of an activity. Real-life parallels are all those rules of behaviour which individuals may regard as applying to them, or not, depending on the circumstances. Thus 'Don't Walk' signs are there for everyone to obey, but may be disobeyed by someone impatient to proceed.

Such 'people' or 'mindset' rules are not immutable and, at times, may exist entirely within the thought processes of those who obey them. They are therefore far less visible but add greatly to the complexity of a game as participants use them to cope with the 'mini-world' they're in. These latter rules are often the subject of intense debate during the debriefing. It is these rules that games can help to uncover. Individuals learn about the effect which such internalised perceptions can have in shaping particular habits or behaviour patterns. When they observe the results of their behaviour during a game, they are often able to appreciate the real-life effect of similar behaviour. This can, in turn, lead to increased self-awareness, and even help to support efforts at behavioural change. Such an outcome may even be the reason for using a game in the first place.

Roles

In real life people have a variety of roles to play. Such roles can help to define behaviour in particular settings: thus, at home—'mother'; at work—'manager'; at university—'pupil'; and on

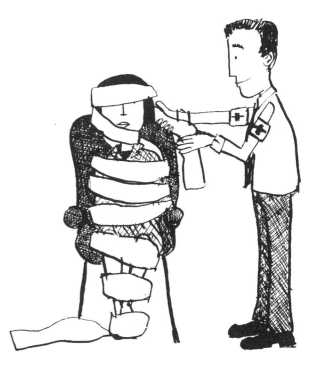

the weekends—'volunteer ambulance officer'. In an activity each player is usually given one role appropriate to the scenario. These roles can be allocated in a variety of ways. The scenario may be described and then players are asked to select and define roles appropriate for themselves within it. Written information may be given to help participants 'get inside' particular roles required for the game, or the Director may merely tell players: 'You are yourselves acting in an environment different to your usual circumstances.' The easiest to use role descriptions give the outline of the required behaviour but leave the participant free to devise the means of putting the role into practice—including such things as the motivations and background of the 'role' they are playing.

The recording process

This is the final element in a game and the one that ties all the action together. It is the process whereby the Director, observers and players keep a record of what is happening. It may be a scoring system, a completed model or only the recollection of events as they occurred. These records form the basis of the debriefing which occurs at the end of each game. Often a designer will suggest the use of 'observers' to assist in ensuring that the various elements are carefully recorded and available for comment during the debriefing. Sometimes a video recording of the action can be used to help remind participants of their own behaviour during an activity, and it can help in times of dispute about such things as 'which action happened when?' or 'who said what to whom?'.

SOME USEFUL QUESTIONS AND HELPFUL ANSWERS

Simulations and games have great potential for enhancing the quality of learning in workplace contexts. How can facilitators ensure they use them effectively and efficiently? What are necessary preconditions to ensure this kind of learning process works, as intended, to create desired outcomes? Is there a core body of knowledge that facilitators of simulations and games need to understand?

1. How can facilitators ensure that they use simulations and games effectively and efficiently?

Take the time to understand the activity thoroughly

Use a 'walk through' as a substitute for completing the activity:

- set the materials out as if you were running the activity;
- walk from place to place;
- stand in each one and place yourself in the players' shoes;
- while you stand there identify questions, etc. about what might happen;
- remain there long enough to record things that come to mind;
- walk around and note the questions, etc. that arise as you do so;
- develop possible answers/comments about all the things you think of;
- spend some time recognising that you cannot anticipate everything;
- allow yourself the luxury of remaining unprepared about some things!

Keep a record of both 'good' and 'bad' experiences

- Keep a journal to assist your memory.
- Make notes immediately after each activity about how it went this time.
- Record particular 'stories' that help to illustrate points that each activity can help you make. These stories can be used on occasions when a particular presentation does not produce the items you were expecting, yet you still need to make them evident to others.
- Arrange such notes in some kind of category list—for example:
  - stories about individual activities;
  - outcomes of several iterations of the same activity;
  - ways in which individuals responded to particular aspects of activities;
  - how different types of groups responded to particular activities.

Take the time to reflect on your own performance

- Have a critical friend attend some activities and give you feedback on your management of the activity. Use their observations to shape and enhance your next performance, and then reflect on any changes or differences.

- Tape-record some of your own 'briefing' and 'debriefing' sessions, then transcribe these and look for helpful (and unhelpful) comments you make.
- Video-tape the entire process and then observe yourself in action. Identify times when you seem to be 'in tune' with the group, or when you seem to be unaware of things that are occurring in front of you. One of the editors did this recently and, during the playback session, saw behaviours, entirely unobserved during the session, which had had a very powerful impact on other participants. Because these actions went unnoticed and were not commented on, at least one person did not receive feedback which could have influenced their future behaviour, and the entire process was less successful than expected. The lesson was well learnt: both editors now watch even more carefully and take the time to ask for explanations of behaviours and comments which seem 'out of sync' with what they have observed.

2. Are there necessary preconditions to ensure these kinds of learning activities work as intended, and create the desired outcomes?

There are many occasions when such an activity is not appropriate, and just as many when it could be an inspired choice for encouraging learning. The choice is yours as leader and teacher.

Issues of timing

- Do you have enough flexible time? Participants seldom comply with prior notions of timing, especially when an activity is open-ended. Flexible scheduling tactics are vital. All the designers have provided suggested 'times', but they are not to be taken as absolute. Their estimates were based on particular groups and learning contexts; your settings will be different, and your participants may be smarter (or slower) than those encountered by the designers.

Issues of logistics

- Do you have enough of the right materials? Murphy's Law definitely applies in games! Always have more than you need and check that everything you need is complete, and then be prepared to find that it is not when the game begins.
- Do you have the right setting? Clear, open spaces and mobile furniture are always best. Plenty of room is essential. Don't play games next to the school chapel during service, or next to the principal's office while he or she is in residence, unless you have given everyone plenty of warning and there is no alternative.

Issues of purpose

- Do you know what the game can do? Practice and personal experience are the best guides here. Discuss your needs with those who are experienced. Do a 'walk through' practice: think about yourself in each role. Handle all the materials. But most of all try and let your imagination fly, because the real issue here is: 'What can the players do with the game?'
- Do you know what you want the game to do? One game can do many things. And many games can achieve the same objective. It is critical to know clearly what direction you want it to pursue, even if the players do take it somewhere else!
- Is your purpose still relevant to the group's learning—as the time to begin approaches? Some games continue to be apt regardless of the development of the group's learning. Others become simply irrelevant, or even counter-productive. When you are near the time to begin, check again—and have a standby ready—just in case. *Never* proceed just because it is 'in the program'.

People issues

- Are the underlying cultural values and norms acceptable to the players? Games are designed by people who have absorbed the values and norms of their own culture. Some are able to design games compatible across many cultures, some are not. Read the game material carefully to assess the extent to which the concept and materials may need to be amended. If there is too much amending required, select a different game.
- Are the players ready and able to gain learning from the experience? This is a matter of 'readiness', with all the attendant problems this implies. Successful use requires caution and care. Proper briefing can enhance group 'readiness'. Use this step carefully.
- Does the 'games concept' and the theme of the chosen game suit the organisational ethos? Some organisations are attuned to experience-based learning processes. Others are not. Check carefully before you begin. Your credibility as a trainer may be 'on the line'.

3. Is there a core body of knowledge that facilitators of simulations and games need to understand?

The following notes provide a very brief overview of the essential knowledge needed to understand the basic characteristics and parameters of simulations and games.

The earliest known games are recorded on the walls of Egyptian tombs and are probably 4000 years old. These were board games and seem to have been as popular then as Monopoly is now. Some ancient board games were clearly regarded as representing real-life situations and having magical or religious significance. Others were purely for entertainment. Their educational significance is not known.

Chess and Go are two board games which survive from these early times. They are descendants of a game which originated in India. In this game the two groups of figures represented the armies of two warring princes. Their transformation over the centuries into quite dissimilar games reflects some of the cultural differences between West and East. Chess and Go are no longer real representations of battle; however, they still reflect the thought processes of each culture. The learning to be gained from them is reflected in the language of both cultures.

Board games and play items, such as jigsaw puzzles, enjoyed renewed interest in the nineteenth century. However, in most Western countries, education was seen as a serious enterprise and games were not regarded as helpful. They remained, on the whole, outside the schoolroom, while being very popular for entertainment. Surprisingly enough, in the same era, military forces in various European countries—notably Germany, Russia, France and England—were rediscovering the combative elements of games such as Chess and Go and inventing their own 'war games' to reduce the cost of preparing for war. While wars were as fashionable as ever, they had become more expensive. Military commanders turned to two methods of trialling their preparations for war.

The first involved the use of elaborate 'sandboxes' and model soldiers. Battles were 'fought' according to strict and elaborate rules. The aim was to forecast the outcome of various hypothetical battle scenarios. Fans of the 1970s TV drama series called *Callan* will be familiar with the miniature soldiers and the often elaborate sandbox sets used to represent battle sites. The other method adopted by the military involved the conduct of 'exercises' in the field. These aimed to trial soldiers and equipment up to, but short of, the point of actual combat. Such exercises were seen as a time when both soldiers and commanders could try out manoeuvres, skills and equipment without incurring heavy losses.

By the beginning of the twentieth century 'war games' were a regular feature of military training. Their design and implementation became a highly refined. In fact, to avoid the terrible results of 'war by attrition', one of the horrors of the 1914–18 conflict, military strategists 'gamed' many of the major campaigns of 1939–45.

These strategists developed extensive skills in design and application of the materials which they variously referred to as: games, exercises and simulations. And they were quick to see ways in which their skills and materials could be adapted to the peacetime environment. Major American business education centres, such as those at Yale and Harvard, had been using case studies to provide their students with a taste of the real world. After 1945 they were made aware of the much more realistic effects which could be provided by well-designed business simulations and games.

The impact of these materials coincided with the arrival of 'human relations' training including T (or Training) Groups, Encounter Groups, and so on. The idea of being able to practise desirable new behaviours in a low-threat environment was most appealing. So games and simulations were adopted (and adapted) by the human relations trainers and began finding their way into supervisory, public relations and sales training.

By the late 1960s a wide array of materials—and types of materials—was available. The military had substituted computers for their sandboxes, but still conducted regular field exercises. Yale and Harvard had expanded case studies in sophisticated, large-scale representations of selected realities. Assessment Centres had refined 'in-basket' exercises to provide a set formula adopted far and wide. Human relations training had been expanding its influence and was influential in (or influenced by) the experimental approach to adult learning as expounded by Malcolm Knowles. He began to promote the concept of adult learning, as distinct from more familiar theories of learning, based on research into children's learning behaviours and has published extensively, beginning with his book *The Adult Learner—A Neglected Species* (Gulf Publishing Co., 1973).

The widely used Pfeiffer and Jones manuals began to appear at the end of the 1960s. Their *Annual Handbooks for Group Facilitators* have provided many Australian trainers with their first introduction to both the documentation for human relations training and the instructions for a wide variety of activities. The term 'structured experiences' is used by the editors of these annual publications to cover a wide array of activities which fall within the framework of simulations and games as learning activities.

During all this time the Europeans had also developed their skills, although along rather different lines. In general terms, the Americans were concerned with one-to-one and small group interrelations. The English, Dutch, French and Germans were, in general, developing large group, organisational and impersonal strategies and materials. At this time, the research techniques known as 'Nominal Group Technique' and 'Force Field Analysis' were being developed to collect and evaluate data in a highly impersonal mode which, nevertheless, represented possible forms of real behaviour.

During the 1970s the various strands described here mingled, separated and mixed again. The number of games and simulations increased almost exponentially. There were few guidelines for the use of what could be potentially explosive material. There was even less training available. And there were relatively few trainers who could tolerate the thought of surrendering class control to the students. Nonetheless the materials survived and prospered. Books and games suitable for Australian use are still relatively few and far between, but they do exist. A bibliography of Australian materials (produced in 1982) had almost a thousand entries, gathered from around the country. And, as the influence of experiential education strategies filters into training classrooms, there is a need to provide practical examples of theories in action. No other learning process can provide this experience as well, or as inexpensively, as simulations and games.

A spectrum of related simulation techniques

John Taylor and Rex Walford, in the book *Learning and the Simulation Game* (Holt, Rinehart & Winston, Sydney, 1972), provided a useful explanation of the spectrum of techniques, and their ideas form the basis of these comments. The materials all have some relationship with reality; however, their specific relationship is directly in proportion to the amount of 'representative' elements which they contain. The substitution of 'game elements' for real or hypothetical components of our world is a crucial aspect of gaming. The degree of reality afforded by these 'representations' will be used here to locate various types of materials along a scale ranging from 'most real' to 'least real'.

1. The most 'realistic' forms of simulation are *case studies*. They were developed by the Harvard Law School and are 'short story' expositions of particular circumstances which require analysis and discussion. Problem situations are described and suggestions are sought on ways to resolve them.

2. The next most realistic forms are known as *in-baskets* or *in-trays*. In these exercises each player receives the same set of correspondence and messages which must be dealt with by the end of a set period. The objective is to produce behaviour that could be expected on the job. With this form interest has widened to an examination of how the task is carried out.

3. The third step on the spectrum, moving towards a greater degree of abstraction, is the *incident process* (also known as *action-maze*). In contrast to the case study, players using these materials initially receive limited

information. They then acquire more information, depending on the decisions they make on the basis of what they know. Interest is on the data collection, as well as the decision-making process.

4. Socio-drama and psychodrama are related techniques. Role-playing approaches drama or 'play acting' in its use of mock performances to represent certain human interactions. The interest here is on the development of 'natural' responses in a safe learning environment. The aim is to examine how such responses occur, as well as identify ones that can be tried out in 'real life'.

5. Most of the activities in this book are commonly called *simulation games*, and have moved beyond a direct representation of interactions towards the creation of hypothetical environments within which one or more events take place. They combine a higher degree of structure than 'role-playing', with a gradual accumulation of data (through player interaction) as is used in the 'incident process'. The term *structured experience* is also used to describe this kind of activity.

6. The most abstract form of simulation/game is that based on computers or machines. Paradoxically, such a great degree of abstraction can yet produce the greatest appearance of reality. This can be seen in such things as the very sophisticated flight simulators which are available today. Another example is the 'sinking machine' in which Australian sailors can actually experience many of the effects of a sinking ship, and get very wet in the process!

SOME GENERAL COMMENTS TO HELP YOU PREPARE

When introducing these activities, the first (and most important) step is to have confidence in yourself. Confidence will derive both from within yourself and from help you have received from others. Self-efficacy increases with small successes. And confidence determines how much you believe in your own ability. Begin with rehearsals with friends, or with small, short activities whose content and purpose you understand well. If you have never presented a simulation or game before, do not attempt to present one to a large group of learners in the midst of a busy timetable. This can be a recipe for disaster.

Once you have decided to use a simulation, do the following:

Prepare

Have all the materials ready (always have more than you think you'll need, because they have the strangest habit of suddenly disappearing just as you need them). Arrange the materials around the room and stand back and see where they all are. Stand in each place that will be occupied by participants and look around the room to see what they will see.

Practise

Ask your friends to help you rehearse. In this respect simulations and games activities are just like a play. Rehearsal gives you opportunities to observe how the action unfolds. It helps you to anticipate what could happen and it prepares you for all the unexpected things that are never written down, no matter how carefully the designers have 'road-tested' their instructions. It also begins the process of developing stories about what has happened in the game previously.

Think about yourself positively

Just like an audience at a theatre, participants can sense when you are nervous and may become unsettled themselves. Stand tall and be still. Don't prowl around the room—it can make people feel very uneasy. Speak clearly, but never shout. If the group is noisy, hold up your hand for silence. It may take a minute or two for everyone to stop talking, but your voice is ready for action. Just as their murmurs are trailing away, you have control (when you need it) to direct the action, and you can give the control back to the participants quickly because you have not had to first win a shouting match to be heard.

Have faith in the participants

People are almost always keen for you to do well. After all, it is their learning that you are guiding. The better you are, the more they will gain. Demonstrate this faith. Give praise, be careful to acknowledge all comments, answer all questions, but be aware of the following problem.

Beware: When an answer can cause an activity to 'fail'

For achievement of their learning goals, some activities depend on the clever way in which key factors have to be discovered during the course of the action. Some people will ask questions whose answers will reveal too much too soon about what is intended to be discovered during the action phase. When these types of questions are asked, try one of these responses:

- 'That is a very good question. Now what else did people want to ask?' (You have been polite and responded—you just haven't answered them!)
- 'I could answer that question, but I have been known to tell fibs about it, and you wouldn't want me to lie to you, would you?'
- 'I'll have to think about that and get back to you. Next?' (But don't return to that question!)

Trust the designers

All these designs have been tested and they will do what is claimed. Your task is to select the right activity, know how it will work, and then introduce it in a manner that ensures that participants understand what is expected of them. Read all instructions carefully.

Trust the process

Participants are keen to be successful. They will check on what is required and will carry through with the action. They seldom need you to tell them what to do once the action has begun. Sometimes they may even resent your interference! Remember, the process has been designed. It has reason and strength, and will support serious learning. Have fun and allow it to blossom.

ABOUT OUR CATEGORIES

Category 1: Trust, change and solving problems

Trust is something people find difficult to talk about. For some, it may be a taboo subject or emotionally troubling to discuss. When we communicate with others, we cannot readily know whether they base their trust philosophy on the principle of trusting everyone until proven otherwise—or the belief that they must trust no one until proven otherwise. Often we learn too late the importance of trust. Once lost, it is hard to regain. We can't live comfortably, happily or contentedly without trust. For example, we trust that the pilot of our jet aircraft will fly safely; we trust that the bus driver knows the route; and we trust that cars on a speeding freeway will stay in their correct lanes. At work, we trust that those with whom we work will do their jobs properly.

However, we don't often remember to check on whether our trust is well founded; nor do we think to thank others when they have proved to be trustworthy. The activities included in this category help participants to understand why trust is important.

In today's workplace, *change* is a part of life and is inevitable. We need to trust that change is for the better. Knowing how to adjust for change helps everyone accept what is necessary, and also helps them to ask appropriate questions about particular changes that are being proposed. As people get older they may resist change more, or may finally begin to see goals they have hoped to achieve coming nearer. In either case change may still be uncomfortable. The activities in this category may help individuals reflect on their own personal response to approaching changes and guide them in developing effective personal management strategies for accepting, adapting to or resisting them.

When we *solve a problem*, we have also created a change and, in turn, good solutions to difficult problems can lead to higher levels of change management and more difficult problems to solve! As learning facilitators, we are in the business of developing trust, helping others to manage change and gain in their capacity to solve problems. We are also developing our own skills to coach about aspects of change to our own behaviour, knowledge and/or attitudes. These activities can provide us with meaningful and light-hearted ways to support these important processes.

Category 2: Frame games

The frame games in this book were created by using particular combinations of ideas and processes that (we believe) are self-evident enough for others to adapt them for use in a variety of different contexts.

Perhaps your most urgent question is: 'How can I learn about changing, adapting, dismantling (pulling apart), choosing, selecting and designing appropriate games?' As a starting point, we suggest that you look at the structure of the games in this category as though they are a framework or skeleton. Imagine all the games you have ever played since childhood: Monopoly, Scrabble, 101 versions of catch, or skipping, Trivial Pursuit, Snakes and Ladders, Dungeons and Dragons, Chess and jigsaws, just to name a few. Consider every card game you have ever made up or played. These and other games and simulations have been translated and used all around the world.

For example, Snakes and Ladders was developed as a representation of the Hindu concept of the journey of the soul through life to Nirvana (heaven). The snakes represent temptation and a fall from virtue; the ladders represent virtuous acts, which shorten the number of reincarnations on the journey to Nirvana. In Snakes and Ladders, we see the effects of chance on human actions. Chance may be defined as an arbitrary ordering of events determined by some external factor represented by some action, such as the rolling of the dice. In such games, the players accept what destiny allots, without being able to influence the course of events.

What is the skeleton that supports each of the games in this category? What are the rules, roles and other elements that contribute to particular outcomes?

Within each game, a set of mechanics leads players to function in various ways, guides their reactions to given situations and to each other, and prompts them to pursue certain goals within specific boundaries. These mechanisms make up the bones that define the skeleton, or the supporting elements, of the framework of each different activity. They may have been disguised as a part of the boundaries for all players, for individuals or specific situations at strategic times within each game.

These mechanisms make certain things happen. For example, the 'chance' factor in Monopoly contributes an 'unpredictability' mechanism: a 'what if' option or an opportunity to increase or decrease the resources of a particular player or accelerate the game itself.

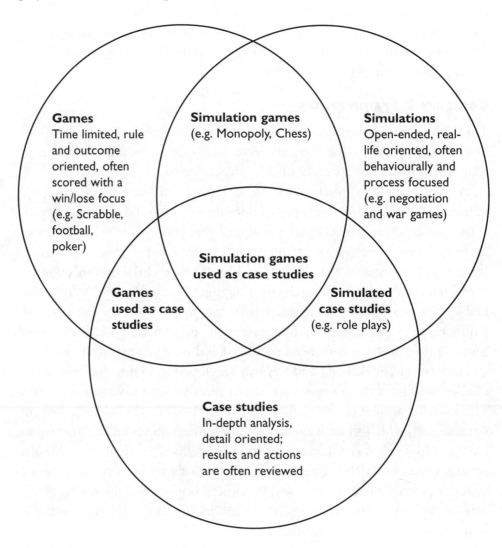

A conceptualisation of games, simulations and case studies, based on the work of Henry Ellington in Ellington, H. et al 1982, A Handbook of Game Design, Kogan Page, UK.

Games
Time limited, rule and outcome oriented, often scored with a win/lose focus (e.g. Scrabble, football, poker)

Simulation games (e.g. Monopoly, Chess)

Simulations
Open-ended, real-life oriented, often behaviourally and process focused (e.g. negotiation and war games)

Simulation games used as case studies

Games used as case studies

Simulated case studies (e.g. role plays)

Case studies
In-depth analysis, detail oriented; results and actions are often reviewed

The more you practise and train your mind to identify the functional mechanisms in all kinds of activities, even while working or playing with children, the more knowledge you gain to help you construct activities of your own. You can train yourself to observe behavioural outcomes and trace them back to the mechanism which contributed to making them happen.

The eight categories used in this book were developed by the editors, but the categories or codes you develop to help recognise mechanisms in games and simulations you encounter can be entirely your own perception. If you recognise a particular outcome as being obtained by any rule, role, function or mechanism in any game, you have begun to construct your own decoding system for taking apart any game, dismantling it so that you can see the structure or skeleton. You'll have found the materials to redesign it, and avenues for adaptation. You will become aware of the reasons for choosing or adapting particular factors to serve your own context or purpose. You'll have developed your own method to adapt any game to suit your own needs for a specialist knowledge game. For example, many of the icebreakers we have included here can have their functional mechanisms rearranged around particular content to illustrate a point and create your own specialist knowledge game.

Category 3: Specialist knowledge and using technology

Unlike the other games in this book, these are not plug'n'play games, unless you have the same context, equipment and aims as those of the designers. You will have to adapt them to make them work. If you examine them closely, however, you will see the mechanisms used, and then be able to use them in parallel contexts. You can combine them with different mechanisms or in the same format as presented here.

Richard East suggests that his game, 'Retail ordering and stock control', can be adapted to suit most retail stores. Principally, this is a game about conducting a detailed analysis of decision-making processes with the use of ordering grids on sheets that contain the specific criteria used for decision making (in this case, ordering apparel). These ordering sheets become tools that are used to trigger discussion on the rationale for each individual decision. When you think about it, the design of the ordering grid could be altered to suit other decision-making situations. In this sense, the structure or skeleton of this game could also make it a frame game.

If the grid is used to initiate discussion and analysis on why things happened the way they did, it is a situation in which a particular problem is analysed. This analysis becomes the goal of the game and the grid is a tool used to solve the problem. In such a context, the game could be termed a problem-solving game.

If the orders are put through a simple book ordering system instead of a computer, is it then no longer a *using technology* game. For that matter, you could look long enough at the structure of each game in this book and find many different categories by which to classify the games.

Category 4: Icebreakers

Icebreakers are games that will warm groups while melting communication barriers. They can set the climate, tone and pace for training, particularly when it will involve active participation in the learning process. You'll find that the icebreaker activities in this book will help participants in any group situation to get to know each other better. With the help of these icebreakers, you can also gain insights into particular groups' needs and goals.

When you have chosen an appropriate icebreaker and used it carefully, you will be able to tap into ways to develop trust among the participants and build rapport with yourself as the facilitator. You may be able to gauge the extent to which participants are open to new experiences, and will know if they are feeling defensive or cautious. Icebreakers can give you indicators as to how active and self-directing you can make your planned activities. Icebreakers can also build momentum for future phases in the training, and assist groups to relax. They help to build group identity and cohesiveness. They're excellent for gaining everyone's involvement. The designers of these icebreakers wanted their activities to encourage people to feel more relaxed by engaging them in meaningful and fun activities.

Managers, co-ordinators, consultants, adult educators, teachers, trainers, facilitators and students can benefit through effective communication using a range of spoken, written, graphic and other non-verbal means of expression. After all, everything we do is communication. We cannot not communicate!

Issues such as past experiences; prior learning; the press and media; our upbringing; our family, friends and their opinions; the country and culture of the place in which we lived during our formative years; religion and personal attitude all influence our aptitude for flexible communication.

Conflict and negotiation during interpersonal communication are affected by inference, intention, hearing, listening and emotions. Some people will see things one way while others will see the same things differently. It is important to have an understanding of the differences and commonality within and between individuals, groups, organisations and societies to achieve common gaols and to demonstrate a knowledge of cultural cohesion and diversity.

You'll find the games and simulations in this category will encourage and develop attitudinal changes in these areas that may lead to greater understanding and participation.

Category 5: Revision of learning

Revising knowledge is important, but can sometimes be uninteresting, repetitive or even patronising for learners. Where's the fun in that? It is, however, a key to long-term learning. Adult educators know how vital it is to revise learning and consolidate information, and these authors have created innovative ways to help people revise their knowledge and gain an improved understanding of the information they have been studying.

The games and simulations in this book make revising fun. You'll find that they are engaging, challenging and will help people to pay close attention to what they've learnt. The activities encourage people to continue learning. The revision activities included here are also a type of 'frame game' where the framework for the game is detailed, but you plug in your own context specific information.

Once learners have experienced this way of revising their knowledge, they're more inclined to be attentive to new information. The challenge of doing well in the revision games at the end of a day of intensive concentration helps everyone stay focused!

The structure of these games has been especially designed to illustrate specific content. The mechanisms used have been chosen to show certain outcomes, which are indicative of the context within which the designers were working and what they were presenting. The challenge for the designers was to make their particular specialist knowledge interesting to learn. It was their way of making mundane, but essential, information interesting. These activities were created to demystify specialist knowledge by using a 'games' framework.

Unless you have an identical situation, you will not be able to take these games and run them without reinterpreting them into your own context.

Category 6: Communication, conflict, negotiation and cultures

Having the 'best of intentions' is seldom enough to help anyone really understand the forces motivating others. Sometimes we are not fully aware of the reasons why we behave in certain ways at particular times. Yet it is important to understand these powerful but intangible forces if we are to take action, identify choices and make decisions in situations where conflict, compromise and co-operation appear equally possible.

The activities included in this category were designed by adults concerned about supporting the important process of learning how to find, or create, resolutions to problems in modern workplaces and other human communication contexts. Each activity has scope for adaptation to a variety of contexts.

We learn to speak—to communicate—almost from birth. Yet each of us has a unique set of influences shaping our understanding and capabilities for communicating effectively. Did you know that there are half a million words in English—before we begin to count the words in all the other human languages!—and that none of them has only one meaning? Moreover every culture has its own set of gestures, movements and signals—often referred to as 'body language'.

From this vast array of tools, each person selects particular combinations to communicate their meaning. Just think of the complexity involved in the task of achieving 'shared meaning' about anything. These activities identify particular aspects of the complexity involved in human communication and invite participants to reconsider their responses in times of stress and challenge. The game designers observed human behaviour closely, and found ways to provide participants in their activities with experiences that replicate communication and conflict problems.

No one can 'make' us feel things. Yet there are often times when we experience emotions and responses that seem to be triggered by things outside us. The carefully crafted structure of these activities builds a safe environment within which individuals can trial new and different actions. They may also help participants experience unexpected responses to their usual behaviour to help them understand how others perceive them.

Communication, conflict, negotiation strategies and cultural characteristics are factors so integral to our lives that we often have no direct understanding of how they are operating in our lives. These activities will help you introduce your learners to various settings in which they may—however unintentionally—contribute directly to events that reproduce the kinds of conflict they see around them. The notes provided in the 'Learning opportunities' section for each activity provide you with clear guidelines to help in selecting the one which best suits a particular set of needs or goals. As with all the other activities, each one may also produce unexpected outcomes. Of all the activities in this book, these ones require the most careful attention to preparation for the debriefing. Allow extra time for the discussion, accept that some people may wish to resist the results of their own behaviour; do not insist that your observations and responses (or anyone else's) are the 'right interpretation'. Each of us experiences our own lives in our own ways.

Helping others to learn more about themselves involves:

• encouraging everyone to listen and ponder;
• asking questions to open up dialogue and support debate; and, above all,
• suspending our own judgments about others.

In this way you enable participants to leave the experience more thoughtful about themselves, and more aware of the factors that create diversity, difference and the wonderful complexity of human nature.

Category 7: Planning and organising

If, like one of the editors of this book, your participants find planning and organising a difficult and painful process, they may find these activities helpful in reducing their tension and resistance to becoming organised.

Such resistance and difficulties may be linked to the kinds of people we are. Research on learning and on human nature indicates that our uniqueness produces differences which cluster around certain characteristics. While each of us is unique, we share some characteristics with others who are 'like us' in some particular ways. One of the editors is well organised, with a well structured approach to tasks involving minute detail, and was able to face the task of editing this book with equanimity and a passion for being correct in every detail. The other finds such a task near impossible, without a great deal of support, although that person has other strengths. Combining our differences ensured the completion of this book when either of us, working alone, would have found it 'too hard'.

The 'planning and organising' activities included here are intended to help people learn more about their own preferences and understand the value of combining differences to achieve outcomes that go beyond those which are possible when we rely on our own strengths and ignore our weaknesses.

The concept of 'lifelong learning' suggests that we are 'never too old to learn'. And these activities provide tools for you to 'teach older dogs new tricks' so they can use them to plan and organise their work.

Category 8: Energisers

This final category of the simulations and games activities is intended to provide fun and energetic ways to stimulate creativity, learning potential and participants' engagement with the content of your courses.

These activities are mostly quite simple to run, and need less debriefing than those in other categories. Their purpose—as the category title suggests—is to energise and encourage involvement. Each one can be used in a number of ways, and at different times in longer courses. 'Energisers' can include specific course content, or simply be presented as a time for having fun and taking attention off the mental exertions involved in learning and putting it into physical effort. Engaging 'the whole person' is a vital part of ensuring that your efforts as an adult educator are successful. 'Time out' to move around, stand back from the thinking effort, and use all their other muscles and organs, is a constructive and powerful method for helping people to become familiar with new knowledge and skills.

In your training programs allow time for physical activity: give people time to walk around and take their attention off the materials you are presenting, and use these activities to renew their energy and commitment to their own learning.

LOOK-UP MATRIX

Game	Page number	Trust, change and solving problems	Frame games	Specialist knowledge and using technology
1. How to hit a moving hedgehog	35	✓		
2. World peace	43	✓		
3. Learning to learn (LTL)	49	✓		
4. Boarding pass to the New World	52	✓		
5. Trust me	55	✓		
6. Team resources	57	✓		Designing games
7. Problems up and down	62	✓		Landscaping
8. Consensiball	71	✓		
9. Circle of safety	73	✓		
10. Bridging the gap	76	✓		
11. Chaordic construction	79	✓		
12. Playground	87	✓		
13. RiftRaft Inc.	94	✓		Workplace learning
14. Personal learning outcomes—tropical style!	100	✓		
15. Mars huts	103	✓		Customer service
16. Any noise annoys an oyster	109	✓		
17. Territorial terrain	116	✓		
18. 'What would you know?'	120	✓		
19. How to be an egg-spert!	128	✓		
20. Whose rules are these anyway?	134	✓		
21. Where is it?	138		✓	
22. Get it? Do it!	140		✓	
23. Recapping review	145		✓	
24. Rallycross	147		✓	
25. Learning organisation	155		✓	Organisational behaviour/learning
26. What is it?	160		✓	Computer networks
27. The essence	162			Aromatherapy
28. Retail ordering and stock control	165			Retail management
29. Irish preferences	169			Personality types
30. Approaching safety	172			Occupational safety
31. What *bugs* you about a meeting?	179			Meetings
32. Coloured names	183			
33. Say hullo	185			
34. Famous faces	187			
35. Getting to know you	189			
36. Whom am I meeting?	193			
37. Stand on the line—scattergram	196			
38. Coloured shapes	202			
39. CARP (clarify and reinforce points)	206			
40. Exploring ethical dilemmas	209			

Icebreakers	Revision of learning	Communication, conflict, negotiation and cultures	Planning and organising	Energisers
		✓	✓	
		✓		
				✓
		✓		✓
✓		✓		
		✓	✓	
		✓	✓	
✓		✓	✓	✓
	✓	✓		
		✓	✓	
		✓	✓	
		✓	✓	
			✓	
✓			✓	
	✓	✓	✓	
		✓	✓	
	✓	✓	✓	
		✓		
		✓	✓	
		✓	✓	✓
			✓	
	✓	✓	✓	
	✓	✓	✓	
	✓	✓		
	✓	✓	✓	
	✓			✓
			✓	
		✓		
	✓	✓		
		✓	✓	
		✓	✓	
✓				
✓				
✓		✓		
✓		✓	✓	✓
✓		✓	✓	
✓	✓	✓	✓	✓
	✓	✓	✓	✓
	✓		✓	
	✓	✓	✓	

KEY TO THE LAYOUT OF EACH ACTIVITY

Description

This section is for your eyes only to help you to decide on the appropriateness of the activity to your goals.

Learning opportunity

This section identifies outcomes that occurred during trials. You may find that additional learning outcomes are also possible. Refer to the 'Process' section to determine if/when to announce the statements in this section.

Audience

This section describes the kinds of people or groups for whom the activity may be appropriate.

TIME   x hour

All entries in this section are guidelines only.

GROUP SIZE x

This section usually recommends upper and lower limits for numbers of participants.

Resources

This section lists all the items that you must have available before commencing the activity.

Setting

This section identifies minimum environmental requirements.

Briefing

This section generally explains how to introduce the activity to the participants.

Process

This section describes step by step the sequence of events during the action.

Debriefing

This section may suggest questions to ask participants or approaches to take when reviewing the learning.

1

How to hit a moving hedgehog

ALISON HENDERSON AND BRIAN HENNESSY

Description

A team-based activity modelling the kind of disruptive events that create interruptions to work routines and cause emotional stress and dysfunctional behaviour.

The session is best run with at least 2 facilitators and in conjunction with some theoretical input on change management.

Learning opportunity

- To provide participants with an opportunity to assess how they respond to abrupt changes at work.
- To experience and observe how unexpected changes interfere with routine behaviour.
- To form the basis for discussion about effective methods for introducing necessary changes to functional work groups.

Audience

Anyone involved with change, and needing to explore related issues, could participate.

Participants experiencing resistance to change who may also be analysing the processes of change, building effective teams and creating learning organisation paradigms can help illustrate many aspects of change management.

Resources

You'll need:

- Enough identical puzzles to have 1 for each group. The puzzles must be types that groups can work on together (e.g. jigsaws of not more than 250 pieces or similar puzzles such as memory tests, or three-dimensional

TIME **1 hour**

At least 1 hour:
- 20 minutes for puzzle solving
- 40 minutes for feedback and debriefing

GROUP SIZE **12**

At least 12 people (4 groups of 3) are best for group dynamics. The number of groups is flexible, but must be even (i.e. 4, 6, 8, etc. groups). Ideally, the number of members in each group should range from 3 to 7 per group. Additional participants, acting as observers, assist the debriefing.

puzzles). You can also use handmade puzzles made by cutting thick card to form simple jigsaw-type puzzles

- Copies of the 2 observation guides
- Movable tables and chairs
- Whiteboard or flip chart for scribing during the debriefing
- Some chocolates or other small prizes

Setting

Two distinct areas (named the green and blue zones). These can be 2 rooms (but not too far apart) or partitioned sections of 1 room (but not within easy view or hearing range of each other). The groups must be evenly split between the areas. It's best to have the tables and chairs set up the same way in each zone, with each group having its own table with only enough chairs for the participants. Extra chairs must be available around each area, but not at the tables.

Briefing

- Introduce the exercise to all participants while they are together in one area.
- The activity focuses on how groups complete a task and solve problems.
- Distribute observation guidelines to any nominated observers and answer any questions.
- Divide the groups and observers evenly between the green and blue zones. If participants have elsewhere formed groups for other purposes, it is preferable to split them up.
- Each group in each area will be numbered: Green 1 and Green 2, Blue 1 and Blue 2, etc. They are told that they will be timed against all the other groups and that the first group to complete the puzzle correctly will receive a prize.

Process

- Participants move to their designated zones.
- The facilitator for the green zone gives a basic explanation of the puzzle and encourages the groups to work as teams as this will be the best way to solve each puzzle quickly.
- The facilitator for the blue zone also gives a basic explanation of the puzzle to be worked on; however, a designated team leader is appointed to direct activity. Blue zone groups are told that this is seen to be the best way to solve the puzzle quickly.

- All groups commence work on their puzzle solving and timing begins.
- In the green zone, when teamwork develops and/or when a group seems to be solving the puzzle, the green zone facilitator informs the blue zone facilitator.
- In the blue zone, if groups appear to be functioning well in either puzzle solving or team building, the blue zone facilitator informs the facilitator of the green zone.
- Both facilitators tell all groups to stop working on their puzzles.
- In the *green zone*, groups are told that, *because they are doing so well, they are to team up with a group from the other zone, which is struggling a bit with its puzzle.*
- In the *blue zone*, groups are told that the *groups in the other zone are doing well with the puzzle, and that they are to team up with them to boost their numbers, and help them solve the puzzle.*
- Nothing is mentioned about the blue team leaders' new role in this changed format. If there are questions, avoid them politely.

- The groups from the blue zone leave their puzzles and are brought into the green zone, and are assigned a group with which to work. Once assigned, they are told that the timer has been restarted.
- They may wish to move furniture, in which case they are free to do so, but they are not directed to do so. The reformed groups are then allowed to work undisturbed on the puzzle until:
  - one group solves the puzzle;
  - frustrations start to become disruptive; or
  - 20 minutes of puzzle-solving time have elapsed.
- The tables containing the puzzles are brought to the front of the green area, and the participants are encouraged to move their chairs for feedback and discussion.

Debriefing

- Observers are invited to comment on the processes.
- Comments are written up by one of the facilitators, without criticism, in front of the group.
- Group members are allowed to vent their frustrations and feelings, and the words and phrases used are written down by one of the facilitators, without comment.
- Facilitators lead a discussion on what happened and why people reacted as they did. Use the comments from the board to make links to similar disruptive changes that can happen in the workplace or at home. Encourage participants to share experiences of their own to illustrate points about resistance to change and the emotions that can arise.
- Direct discussion towards considering how to facilitate change. Issues of teamwork, group development and competitiveness may arise. At an appropriate moment, introduce the analogy that change can be like a hedgehog: slow but very hard to handle.
- Distribute prizes to each person for participating in the game.

Green zone observation guide

- The groups you are observing are encouraged to form teams to resolve their puzzles.
- They are told that good teamwork is the key to solving their puzzles quickly.

STAGE 1
- Observe how team development occurs (i.e. quickly, slowly, any obvious leaders, etc).

_____

_____

_____

_____

_____

_____

_____

_____

_____

_____

- Just as teamwork starts to develop, group members will be told to stop. They will be told that groups from the other zone are struggling a bit, and that they have to team up with them to help resolve their puzzle. The groups in the other zone have been assigned a team leader and have been told that this is the best way to resolve the puzzle. They have been told that the groups they are to join in your zone are doing well with the puzzles, but that they are being brought in to boost the numbers to solve the puzzles more quickly.

Green zone observation guide

STAGE 2

- Observe the reactions of both groups to the disruption in their puzzle-solving process. Observe how they resolve differences to continue with the puzzle-solving task. These reactions may be verbal or non-verbal. Differences may not be resolved. If so, observe how the initial reactions develop. Note any evidence, relevant to resistance to change, facilitating a change process, team building and group work.

_____

_____

_____

_____

_____

_____

_____

_____

_____

_____

- You'll be invited to feedback these observations to the whole group at the end of the game. You may then divulge how the groups were given different information about their respective progress, and share your observations about stages of group development, etc.

Blue zone observation guide

- The groups you are observing are encouraged to form teams to resolve their puzzles.
- They are assigned a team leader and told that this is the key to solving their puzzles quickly.

STAGE 1
- Observe how team development occurs (i.e. quickly, slowly, how the leaders acted, etc.).

_____

_____

_____

_____

_____

_____

_____

_____

_____

_____

- After a period they will be told to stop and that groups from the other zone are doing well, and they are to team up with them to boost their numbers and help them solve the puzzle. The groups in the green zone have developed a leaderless team and have been told that this is the best way to resolve the puzzle. The groups in the green zone have been told that the groups joining them are struggling with the puzzles, but that their numbers will help solve the puzzle more quickly.

Blue zone observation guide

STAGE 2
- Observe the reactions of both groups to the disruption in their puzzle-solving process.
- Observe how they resolve differences to continue with the puzzle-solving task. These reactions may be verbal or non-verbal. Differences may not be resolved. If so, observe how the initial reactions develop.
- Note any evidence of resistance to change, facilitating a change process, team building and group work.

_____

_____

_____

_____

_____

_____

_____

_____

_____

_____

- You'll be invited to feedback these observations to the whole group at the end of the game. You may then divulge how the groups were given different information about their respective progress, and share your observations about stages of group development, etc.

2 World peace

LANA KUCZYNSKI

Description

A team-based activity using concepts of 'world peace' and 'causes of conflict' to provide opportunities for negotiation, planning for future events, managing conflict and understanding the power of 'hidden agendas', personal communication strategies and unacknowledged group norms.

Learning opportunity

• To learn about issues involved in developing trust among individuals and groups while negotiating for peace and missile disarmament.

Audience

Any situation where people need to deal with each other, negotiate and/or learn to trust the people with whom they're dealing.

Resources

You'll need:

• Sealed envelopes, each containing 1 set of instructions as provided on the following pages
• Prepared boxes of matches with each match representing 1 missile
• Name tags or labels, pens and paper for each participant

Setting

Three regions with separate rooms or space, not within easy hearing range of each other.

TIME 2.5 hours

Approximately 2.5 hours:
• 10 minutes for briefing before the game commences
• 100 minutes (approx.) for the actual game
• 40 minutes for debriefing at the conclusion of the game
  This can more or less depend on the number of participants and the involvement and complexity developed through the game.

GROUP SIZE 18

Eighteen people (15 who represent countries and 3 who represent regions). If there are more than 18 participants, you can add more countries in each *hot spot* region, but this must be prepared in advance. If there are fewer than 18, you can remove one complete region *or* selected countries, but check that participant instructions don't refer to a country you've removed.

Briefing

- Ask for 3 volunteers to be United Nations Security Council Regional Representatives. Hand each an envelope listing the countries within their region and some instructions.
- Everyone sits around a table with the facilitator (UN Secretary General) explaining the rules to all the representatives.
- Show the whole group a box of matches and demonstrate that when the matches are out of the boxes and standing upright, the missiles are armed. When the matchbox is closed or the matches are returned to the matchbox, the missiles are disarmed. The objective is world peace, but an ignited match represents a devastating bomb blast.
- Explain the following to the participants:
  - The end objective in each region is to have peace and, if possible, total disarmament within 100 minutes from the start of game play.
  - During the game, Regional Representatives can communicate with each other if they wish.
  - Regional Representatives may shuttle between each country within their regions or even swap regions completely—it is up to them. If they decide to swap regions, they aren't allowed to tell the countries in their regions of their plans.
  - Regional Representatives must report to the UN Secretary General with an update of the situation every 20 minutes.
  - Participants can divulge some of the information in the envelopes. They do have hidden agendas, which can be divulged, but only to specific countries with consideration given to the consequences
  - For the sake of the game, it has been established that all countries have agreed that there should be peace in the world. Some countries, however, do not agree that disarmament is the answer to peace. It is up to individual countries to negotiate peace in their regions with other countries directly or through their Regional Representative.
- Give everyone a name tag/label.
- Give the members of the UN Security Council sealed envelopes containing instructions, their country, their region and their missiles.

Process

- Set a game finishing time that leaves a minimum of 40 minutes for debriefing, and allow groups to form and proceed as instructed.
- The facilitator ensures that the game is played according to the rules and within the time. Give advice only if required.

- At appropriate moments, tell regional representatives that the UN is prepared to launch an attack on any country that threatens peace. This information is to be made known only to selected countries at the discretion of the Regional Representatives.
- Approximately halfway through the game, the facilitator reports a news flash to Regional Representatives that 'there have been successful nuclear tests performed by *India in Asia*, *Poland in Europe* and *Egypt in the Middle East*'. It is up to the Regional Representatives how, when or if they inform the countries in their regions.
- The game ends at the allotted time. If peace hasn't been achieved, Regional Representatives can take last minute action. As a last resort, the facilitator as UN Secretary General can make recommendations to any member of the Security Council.

Debriefing

Promote discussion on issues such as:

- What happened and why?
- How did they feel?
- What could have been done differently? When and why?
- How do actions and decisions relate to trust?
- What changed?
- Were there examples of communication barriers or successes?
- Did they observe conflict?
- Was race an issue at any time and, if so, did this affect negotiation?
- How did the group form teams and interrelate?
- How does this correlate with real-life situations?

Region 1 envelopes

REGION 1—UNITED NATIONS SECURITY COUNCIL
Regional Representative from Australia
- You represent the countries in your region: Saudi Arabia, Iran, Libya, Jordan and Israel.
- You can communicate with other representatives at any time.
- You can move among all the countries in your region.
- You can swap regions with another representative but you cannot tell anyone in either region.
- You must report to the UN Secretary General every 20 minutes.

Region 1—United Nations Security Council
Saudi Arabia (with matchbox containing 12 missiles)
- Your country agrees to peace settlement.
- Because you distrust other countries in your region, Saudi Arabia pretends to have only 10 missiles, keeping the other 2 a secret.

Region 1—United Nations Security Council
Iran (with matchbox containing 5 missiles)
- Iran doesn't want to negotiate with other countries, unless through a UN Regional Representative. You distrust, and refuse to deal with, the Australian Regional Representative.

Region 1—United Nations Security Council
Libya (with matchbox containing 12 missiles)
- Your country doesn't want disarmament and believes that peace can be obtained through other ways. You believe that disarmament would lead to war because of lack of trust.
- Libya's secret agenda is to control Iran.

Region 1—United Nations Security Council
Jordan (with matchbox containing 7 missiles)
- Jordan secretly believes that Libya wants to take over Jordan, but you don't want to make this belief public.
- You want to get together with the other countries within your region to form an alliance against Libya.

Region 1—United Nations Security Council
Israel (with matchbox containing 7 missiles)
- Israel believes that, for peace to exist, all countries must destroy their missiles.
- You're prepared to give up territory for peace.

Region 2 envelopes

REGION 2—UNITED NATIONS SECURITY COUNCIL
Regional Representative from Sweden
- You represent the countries in your region: Cambodia, Indonesia, China, Korea and Vietnam.
- You can communicate with other representatives at any time.
- You can move among all the countries in your region.
- You can swap regions with another representative but you cannot tell anyone in either region.
- You must report to the UN Secretary General every 20 minutes.

Region 2—United Nations Security Council

Cambodia (with matchbox containing 12 missiles)
- Your country agrees to peace settlement.
- Because you distrust other countries in your region, Cambodia pretends to have only 10 missiles, keeping the other 2 a secret.

Region 2—United Nations Security Council

Indonesia (with matchbox containing 5 missiles)
- Indonesia doesn't want to negotiate with other countries, unless through a United Nations Regional Representative.
- You distrust, and refuse to deal with, non-Asian Regional Representatives.

Region 2—United Nations Security Council

China (with matchbox containing 12 missiles)
- Your country doesn't want disarmament and believes that peace can be obtained through other ways. You believe that disarmament would lead to war because of lack of trust.
- China's secret agenda is to control Indonesia.

Region 2—United Nations Security Council

Korea (with matchbox containing 7 missiles)
- Korea secretly believes that China wants to take over Korea, but you don't want to make this belief public.
- You want to get together with the other countries within your region to form an alliance against China.

Region 2—United Nations Security Council

Vietnam (with matchbox containing 7 missiles)
- Vietnam believes that all countries must destroy their missiles for peace to exist.
- You're prepared to give up territory for peace.

Region 3 envelopes

REGION 3—UNITED NATIONS SECURITY COUNCIL
Regional Representative from Japan
- You represent the countries in your region: US, France, Germany, UK and Russia.
- You can communicate with other representatives at any time.
- You can move among all the countries in your region.
- You can swap regions with another representative but you cannot tell anyone in either region.
- You must report to the UN Secretary General every 20 minutes.

Region 3—United Nations Security Council

US (with matchbox containing 12 missiles)
- Your country agrees to peace settlement.
- Because you distrust other countries in your region, the US pretends to have only 10 missiles, keeping the other 2 a secret.

Region 3—United Nations Security Council

France (with matchbox containing 5 missiles)
- France doesn't want to negotiate with other countries, unless through a United Nations Regional Representative.
- You distrust, and refuse to deal with, the Scandinavian Regional Representative.

Region 3—United Nations Security Council

Germany (with matchbox containing 12 missiles)
- Your country doesn't want disarmament and believes that peace can be obtained through other ways.
- You believe that disarmament would lead to war because of lack of trust.
- Germany's secret agenda is to control France.

Region 3—United Nations Security Council

UK (with matchbox containing 7 missiles)
- The UK secretly believes that Germany wants to take over the UK, but you don't want to make this belief public.
- You want to get together with the other countries within your region to form an alliance against Germany.

Region 3—United Nations Security Council

Russia (with matchbox containing 7 missiles)
- Russia believes that all countries must destroy their missiles for peace to exist.
- You're prepared to give up territory for peace.

3 Learning to learn (LTL)

JEFF KINDER

Description

A whole group activity, which uses the concept of the 'life cycle' to assist participants to consider learning as an on-going factor in their lives.

Learning opportunity

- To promote discussion regarding the benefits of lifelong learning: why it's both fun and important. For example, constantly changing work environments, the benefits of Recognition of Prior Learning (RPL): delving into barriers to lifelong learning (e.g. closed attitudes), and some techniques for overcoming barriers (e.g. by trusting and learning from each other).

Audience

This simulation suits workplace situations and students in tertiary educational settings where the need for ongoing learning is to be explored.

Resources

Give clear oral instructions, but printed instructions may also help participants.

Setting

Allow enough room for your participants to form a circle. This can be inside or outside and they can sit or stand.

Briefing

Read steps 1, 2 and 3 of the 'Process' to the group.

TIME **1 hour**

One minute per participant, plus 15 minutes for debriefing and discussion. For example, approximately 20 minutes for a group of 5, 25 minutes for a group of 10, etc.

GROUP SIZE 5–10

5–10 participants would be most effective, but the simulation will still work with 3–20 people.

Process

Steps 1, 2 and 3 can be printed as instructions for participants.

1. Form a circle and agree on a person to start. The group/circle is going to simulate lifelong learning. The agreed starting person will behave as if they are 10 years old. The next person (clockwise) will act 20, the next 30, and so on. (If your group has more than 10 people, you may need to consider smaller age increments.)

2. You are a particular stage in human life. You represent a significant learning situation or need for learning that suits your allotted stage or age. For example:

    (a) A 15-year-old may need to learn new ways to be able to interact with adults on a less childish level.

    (b) A 40-year-old may need to learn new technology or change careers when stability would be more comfortable.

    (c) An 80-year-old may need to adapt to new banking arrangements and forgo routine.

3. How do you do it? When it's your turn:
   (a) state your allotted age; then
   (b) show the significant learning situation or need for learning in some creative way. Perhaps by: telling it, showing it, acting it, miming it, drawing or even singing it, rhyming or chanting it.
   (c) Help others to understand your meaning before passing on to the next (clockwise) person.

Encourage the participants to (metaphorically) 'put on glasses with special filtering lenses' and to look at the activity from the perspective of lifelong learning and learning from each other.

Debriefing

- Begin with the statement that you'd like to 'open a door' for participants to continue noticing lifelong learning and continue to trust learning contributions from each other long after the simulation is finished.
- Suggest that those in this training session may bring expectations that training should be neatly packaged and laid on the table on a silver platter for them. They may bring their memories of secondary educational classroom settings and expect a repetition of this. Many may believe that the responsibility for training rests in the hands of their employer. They are being given evidence that life is continual learning. They will need to consider becoming self-motivated, lifelong learners to keep up with change.
- Many have worked through corporate takeovers and mergers. Company restructuring is creating management structures that are more efficient, with fewer positions for those who have climbed the corporate ladder and found a comfortable rung on which to sit. The concept of long-term job security is no longer promised, certainly not without expectations of well-sustained contributions to company productivity. Staff are expected to be increasingly multiskilled. Lifelong learning is part of the process of achieving personal goals.

Boarding pass to the New World

FIONA LOSCHIAVO

TIME 20 min.
Approximately
20 minutes.

GROUP SIZE 5+
From 5 to several
hundred people.

Description

An activity using simple physical exercises to provide a kinaesthetic experience of having to make sudden and unexpected adjustments to familiar movements and knowledge.

Learning opportunity

• To help participants identify behaviour patterns in change management and to develop flexibility to cope with change.

Audience

Any large or small group of people who are considering—or facing—issues of change, communication problems and/or uncomfortable working relationships.

Resources

You'll need a copy of this *New World* translation for each person.

Old	New
Head	Toes
Shoulders	Knees
Knees	Heads
Toes	Shoulders

Setting

An area with enough room for participants to stand or sit well spaced while allowing people to move freely without interference.

Briefing

Explain that to help everyone to loosen up and to enable them to complete the activity to follow, they are to sing a popular chosen children's song with accompanying actions following the movements of the facilitator.

Process

- Slowly sing *Head and shoulders, knees and toes* with actions. The tune is very simple and repeats, but if you don't know it, just follow this rhythm:

1 Head	2 and	3 shoulders	4	5 knees	6 and	7 toes	8
5 knees	6 and	7 toes	8	5 knees	6 and	7 toes	8
1 Head	2 and	3 shoulders	4	5 knees	6 and	7 toes	8
5 We	6 all	7 clap	8	5 hands	6	7 together	8

- The actions are simply to point at your corresponding body parts and then clap. Encourage participation, but don't make this compulsory.
- Conduct a short discussion on the feelings felt by individuals (silly, self-conscious, fun, etc.), but keep it light-hearted.
- Narrate *The New World Story*.

The New World Story

I'm sorry folks, but Earth has been informed that a comet is heading straight for us. The size of this comet is so large that no technology known to human kind has the power to destroy it or alter its path. When it collides with Earth, Earth will be no more. Our only hope is to send an intergalactic SOS and pray that there is another intelligent life form to come to our rescue.

To our delight, it has been discovered that a planet with a very similar environment exists in another galaxy. The inhabitants are of similar appearance to humans and could even be mistaken for Earthlings, except that they all speak English, but with a difference.

Our benevolent intergalactic hosts are sending a fleet of spaceships to rescue us. To avoid possible communication problems and dissension between the new and old inhabitants, our rescuers have requested that one simple entry test be passed before boarding the spaceships.

Now distribute a copy of the *New World* translations to each participant, making sure it remains face down until participants are instructed otherwise.

- State that to eliminate confusion and to aid communication on our new planet, we are all requested to sing our song again with the same words, but pointing to new parts of the body.
- Make it clear that each participant will have 2 minutes in which to memorise the *New World* translations. Instruct participants to turn over their sheets and commence timing, after which the participants are requested to turn their sheets back face down. It is important to ask this once only.
- Now ask everyone to take their boarding pass entry test and lead the singing and actions of *Head and shoulders, knees and toes*. When you try out and practise the new actions for yourself before your session, you'll realise that the changed pattern of actions is not as difficult as it may at first seem. Start very slowly and sing twice, gradually increasing the speed of the song.

Debriefing

- Lead a discussion on feelings and the degree of difficulty of this exercise. Some interesting points come out of an exercise like this. Typical behaviours and responses include:
  - Competitive behaviours: cheating or trying to compete with others instead of securing their own boarding pass.
  - Collaborative behaviours: 2 or more people helping each other.
  - Dysfunctional behaviours: distracting others during the activity by talking, joking or doing bizarre actions.
  - Task oriented: just finishing the exercise, while remaining focused, but without much thinking.
  - Strategic thinking: seeing the whole picture and realising what needs to occur.
  - Process thinking: trying to develop a pattern and/or rhythm.
- Another aspect to draw from group discussion is that, in real situations, people may well act differently. We all too often convert new methods back into old ways of thinking, but when there is no direct match between new and old, it can cause many problems and comments such as 'But we always did it this way before'.

  To be able to enter the New World either via the spaceships or in our ever-changing workplaces, we have to start thinking in the new way without reverting or translating back into the old. This is called making a paradigm shift.

5 Trust me

STEVE RENWICK

Description

A brief physical activity designed to demonstrate the development of an atmosphere of trust.

Learning opportunity

• To demonstrate the benefits of learning to develop trust between teacher and learner, by asking (rather than telling) people to do things.

Audience

All levels of people: from senior managers to people working at the coalface, in blue collar and white collar industries as well as coaching and mentoring environments.

Resources

You'll need 1 chair for each participant.

Setting

Room for participants to turn their chairs upside down.

Briefing

• In this activity, the briefing is almost more important than the debriefing. The more convincing the briefing, the more quickly trust develops and the more likely it is that people will do what they're asked.
• Involve participants in a brief discussion about how we develop trust in one another, and how we can achieve more by asking, rather than telling people, to do things.

TIME 3–5 min.
3–5 minutes for the action, plus extra time for the discussion afterwards.

GROUP SIZE 1+
From 1 to 50 people.

Ask for examples of how we trust others to guide us when we are unsure or trying new things; and of when we know we must move out of our comfort zones to achieve our goals.

• Stress that developing a bond between the teacher and learner is very important.

Process

As you introduce each action, do it yourself once you have described the required action. Ask participants to:

1. trust you by simply doing what you ask them to do;
2. stand beside their chairs and then to turn their chairs upside down;
3. raise their arms above their head and to call out 'trust';
4. reset their chairs and be seated.

Debriefing

Question participants' understanding of what they've just done:

• What's the difference between a request and an order?
• Did people have to move out of their comfort zones?
• What are the benefits of trust?
• How can what they just discussed be put into practice during the training?
• Can this be beneficial during training and at home and work?

6 Team resources

MICHAEL BROAD

Description

An activity to develop an understanding of the requirements for effective facilitation of simulations and games.

Learning opportunity

To demonstrate the:

- importance of careful planning when preparing to run games and simulations;
- indispensable benefits of debriefing activities to identify and reinforce learning outcomes;
- possibly adverse results when a facilitator intervenes inappropriately during the action;
- value of allowing a game to conclude and the possible consequences of not doing so.

Alternatively, the competitive game can be allowed to run to its conclusion and can be useful for practising teamwork and team building, while examining approaches to planning and/or strategic development. This activity can also be a good leadership training activity to explore the impact of abrupt, unexplained changes to work priorities.

Audience

People who are going to be conducting structured experiences and learning activities such as games and simulations. It is helpful if they have had some experience or training in presenting information (e.g. train-the-trainer skills).

TIME 50+ min.

From 50–75 minutes:
- 30–45 minutes for the game (preparation and action)
- 20–30 minutes for the debriefing

GROUP SIZE 8

Any number of teams of 4–8 people as long as there is sufficient space. A minimum of 8 people arranged in 2 teams of 4.

Resources

You'll need:

- At least 1 *Instruction sheet* and the *Team resource map* for each group
- Flip chart paper (butcher's paper) and coloured marker pens
- Whiteboard and pens for the debriefing

Setting

A room large enough to accommodate all the teams, with a lot of space between them so group discussions cannot be overheard. Before beginning the activity, arrange all the participants' chairs in a semicircle facing a whiteboard or flip chart. Once the teams are allocated, participants may take their chairs with them to their work areas.

Briefing

- Announce that: 'In order to explore training games, it can be useful to have a common experience and move on from there.' Say no more about the goals of the activity.
- Divide the group into teams.
- Use whatever prior understanding you have of the characters in the group and organise the teams to create as much competition as possible.
- Give each team a copy of the *Instruction sheet*, the *Team resource map* and some flip chart paper and pens.
- Tell participants that they have 20 minutes to prepare before they do battle as per the *Instruction sheet*.
- Quietly observe the groups to decide if they need more time to prepare before the battle. If extra preparation time is necessary, say nothing, but allow them to continue until you judge that everyone is ready. Then call 'time' for the next step.

Process

- Once the battle starts, watch groups, but say nothing apart from 'speed up a little' if you think this will create more tension and competition.
- When all teams are participating and competition has reached a high point, stop the activity abruptly by saying something like 'I'm sorry, but this really isn't working as other groups have done it. Please all just go back to your original positions.' Be very firm and quite assertive at this point to ensure that everyone returns to their previous places in the semicircle.

• Now begin a short explanation about games and simulations (such as various types, their history and use) as though their game never happened. Pretend to ignore any aspect of the game play.

Debriefing

• At first, people will often try to slip back into the game and/or be concerned about whether they were winning or losing at the time the play was abruptly ended. At other times they may wait, somewhat patiently, for you to give them an opportunity to finish play. Reiterate that play will not continue.

• Now comes the hard part: dealing with their anger. Allow people time to work through their feelings and emotions, during which time you may bear the brunt of some criticism.

• After the participants have spent sufficient time venting their concerns, move the discussion on to what they can draw from their experience in terms of how to (or not to) conduct structured experiences such as games and simulations. Ensure the discussion covers:

  − the difficulties and confusion experienced when an activity is just stopped, as this one was (perhaps time has been insufficiently allocated, a co-presenter or higher authority interrupts proceedings, etc.). In these situations, a lot of emotion is left bubbling inside the participants. These feelings can make it impossible to move on to anything else. Such structured experiences must be allowed to run their course;

  − reasons why people will want to return to the game (sing their anthems, display their flags and/or win the battle);

  − negative feelings towards others when an experiential activity isn't concluded and debriefed properly;

  − confusion about possible 'learning outcomes' because the game didn't finish;

  − better planning to address both time problems and emotional responses.

Instruction sheet

Welcome! You're an integral part of an enthusiastic team and about to compete with other teams to own all the resources!

This game has 2 stages:

1. The preparation

This phase will last approximately 20 minutes. As a group, you have 3 tasks to complete:

(a) Create a team anthem—a chant to rally your troops or a song to motivate spirits for the battle.

(b) Create a team flag to promote your victory.

(c) Mark out your resources on the sheet headed *Team resource map*.

2. The battle

The rules for this stage are similar to another game you may know—Battleship.

(a) Teams draw straws to see who goes first.

(b) The team going first (the attackers) call out a co-ordinate (or grid map location—e.g. D6) to the other team (the defenders).

(c) If there is a portion of a resource at the location called, the defending team must call out 'Strike!'. When this happens, the attacking team calls another grid map co-ordinate (e.g. H9).

(d) A team continues until it misses.

(e) The team that was defending now starts attacking.

(f) When all squares of a resource have been struck, the resource (metaphorically) becomes the property of the attacking team.

(g) Play continues until one team has lost all its resources.

Good luck!

Team resource map

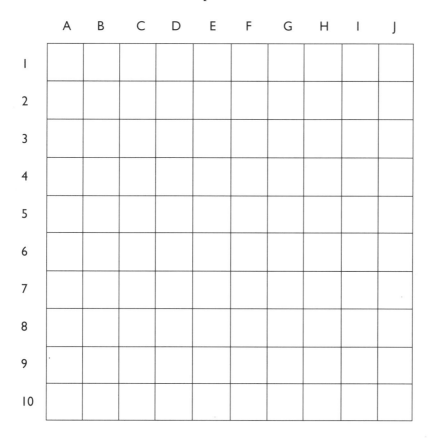

Mark out on the grid the positions for every object (in consecutive squares running vertically or horizontally, not diagonally):
- training room (6 squares)
- training office (6 squares)
- administrative/support staff member (5 squares)
- overhead projector (4 squares)
- computer (3 squares)
- printer (3 squares)
- set of training room desks (2 squares)
- set of training room chairs (2 squares)
- whiteboard (2 squares)

The various resources don't have to touch each other. Here is an example:

7 Problems up and down

ANDREW BOULTON

TIME 90+ min.

From 90–100 minutes approximately as follows:
- 10 minutes to brief participants
- 60 minutes for the action
- 30 minutes for debriefing and evaluation

GROUP SIZE 6–9

From 6–9 participants representing senior positions in a Parks and Gardens Department (e.g. a group of 9 players would have 5 players as the landscape construction team, 1 player as the supervisor and 3 players as observers).

Description

A team-based activity which models typical restraints encountered in hierarchical structures. It also provides ideas for resolving communication problems and improving teamwork and cross-departmental co-operation.

Learning opportunity

This activity demonstrates how management of a work unit can be plagued by problems such as late completion of work or budget overruns—factors which are often caused by more complex issues that are unknown or overlooked.

It can stimulate thought about underlying factors and help in evaluating the nature of specific issues which emerge during the activity. It can help demonstrate the need to establish formal meetings to address similar 'real-life' issues and create solutions, amend current work practices and prepare for further change.

Audience

People working in any form of hierarchical organisation.

Resources

You'll need:

- Model of soil bank as shown on the construction detail sheet (you may need to make adjustments to produce a basic soil bank using materials that you have available)
- 50 matchsticks painted white
- 50 matchsticks painted black
- 50 matchsticks painted brown
- 50 matchsticks painted yellow

- 30 strips of thin green paper or cardboard (2 cm wide x 22 cm long)
- 60 sewing pins (preferably with coloured ends, e.g. dressmaking pins)
- 2 knitting needles
- Scale rule
- Landscape plan (so quantities of materials can be calculated)
- Role description for each player
- Pens and paper for each observer
- Copies of instructions for all players and observers
- Set of task cards, to be distributed as follows:
  Task card 1—given to the Parks and Gardens Supervisor before commencing the activity
  Task card 2—given to the Supervisor when the landscape construction team appear to have the job well under control
  Task card 3—given to the Supervisor towards the end of the process (just as things seem to be OK)

Setting

Two separate rooms containing tables and chairs (one for the Supervisor containing approximately half the material on the resources list and another room for the landscape construction team containing the model of the soil bank). The landscape construction team's room is known as The Site.

Briefing

This activity is based around the building of a model, which is the most important prop in the game/simulation.

- Provide each player with a position description explaining roles (these are best distributed randomly or by having participants choose from a 'lucky dip').
- Provide all observers with pens and paper.
- Show the landscape construction team and some observers to their room.
- Show the Supervisor and some observers to their room.

Process

- Give the Supervisor the *Task card 1* and announce that the process has begun.
- When the Supervisor advises you that there are not enough resources, provide items as requested.
- When the landscape construction team appear to have the job well under control, give *Task card 2* to the Supervisor.
- When the landscape construction team feel they've completed the job, go to the landscape construction team and act as the very dissatisfied president of the football club, Mr Nido Moorbere.
- If they have plants on the top of the soil bank, complain that this is where spectators will stand and that the plants will be in the way.
- If they have planted no plants on top of the soil bank, complain that the spectators will need shade.
- Then give *Task card 3* to the Supervisor.

Debriefing

- Review the action of the game and ensure that all players have a chance to describe the behaviour and reactions they had and saw in others.
- Invite the observers to report on what they heard and saw.
- Ask questions such as the following, to help explore the process:
  - Did all players feel a sense of belonging to the organisation?
  - What helped or hindered this?
  - How did the landscape construction team members feel about having decisions made for them?
  - Who made the important decisions?
  - Was the decision making shared to solve problems?

- Who finally took the initiative to install the erosion/weed control underlay and plant the trees?
- How did the others feel about this?
- What were the reactions and feelings of players when the Supervisor announced the text of each task card?
- Was there conflict between individuals?
- Did anyone feel they were ignored or unfairly treated?
- Did all players fully understand the messages given to carry out the required tasks to complete the job?

• Ask about the relationships with the 'real world':
- Did the game depict a management model that is hierarchically structured?
- To what extent did players use their skills and knowledge individually and collectively as part of a team?
- What role best describes the way players see themselves and their colleagues?
- What methods were used to reach decisions?
- To what extent did each team member find job and self-satisfaction within teams and the organisation?
- Real-life managers are often in the dark about the opinions of the workers who perform day-to-day tasks. Was this evident during the game or simulation?
- How did communication in the game affect the outcome of the job?
- What specific interpersonal communication skills were used (and to what level) to obtain co-operation between players?

Task card 1

MEMO

To: Parks and Gardens Supervisor
From: Parks and Gardens General Manager
Subject: Work to be completed in my absence

The opening of the new football oval we've constructed is on the first Friday of next month. The soil bank needs to be completed. This requires underlay fitted in the usual manner to control erosion and weed growth. After this, the area is to be mass planted: the nursery has set aside 200 plants for this purpose. They want group planting with equal spacings between plants. Another job that is a priority is working out a material quantity list based on the Landscape Plan provided. We must start work on this next week.

Don't forget that everyone's rostered day off (RDO) is the first Friday of next month.

I know I can rely on you and will enjoy my fishing!

PS Don't neglect your regular office duties by spending too much time on site. The majority of your regular office work must continue unhindered!

Explanation of your materials list
Green strips = underlay for erosion/weed control
Sewing pins = steel pegs to hold down underlay
Painted matchsticks represent plants:
Yellow = 0.5 m plants
Black = 1 m plants
Brown = 2 m plants
White = 3 m plants
Knitting needles = spades

Task card 2

The Acting Parks and Gardens General Manager has looked at the job and isn't happy with the progress of work or the style of planting. There is concern it won't be completed on time and will be difficult to maintain over the following years using the existing ride-on mowers.

Task card 3

The president of the football Club, Mr Nido Moorbere, has complained to the landscape team about the number of plants on the top of the soil bank. Team members have passed this complaint on to you because they have no authority to act. You have to find a solution to the problem and keep all parties happy.

Role descriptions

✂ -

Observers 1 and 2

- Your role in this game is to observe the landscape construction team and write down all the problems and issues as you see them.
- You cannot communicate with the team.
- You can communicate with the facilitator, and he or she may (or may not) be able to answer your questions.

✂ -

Observer 3

- Your role in this game is to observe the Parks and Gardens Supervisor, and write down all the problems and issues for the person in this role as you see them occur.
- You cannot communicate with the Supervisor.
- You can communicate with the facilitator, and he or she may (or may not) be able to answer your questions.

✂ -

Parks and Gardens Supervisor

- Your role in this game is to complete the task cards provided to you by the facilitator.
- You can only communicate verbally with the team leader of the landscape construction team.
- You can see the team leader at The Site after the game commences and then only at 15 minute intervals, for no more than 3 minutes.

✂ -

Landscape construction team leader

- You are responsible for the 'duty of care' for your team members and to ensure that the team completes the job on time.
- You can only communicate verbally with each team member and your Supervisor.
- You can communicate with the facilitator and he or she may (or may not) be able to answer your questions.

✂ -

Team members 1, 2 and 3

- Your role in this game is to be responsible to your team leader.
- You can verbally communicate only with other team members and your team leader.

Models of soil bank

These are not to be shown to players until the debriefing.

Model of soil bank prior to commencing game

Model of soil bank after the erosion/weed control underlay has been laid

Completed model of planted soil bank

How to build model of bank

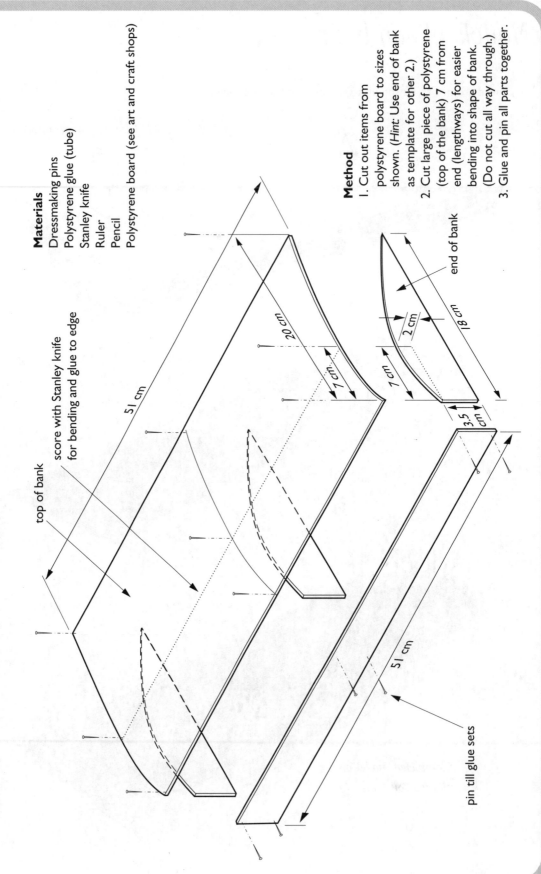

Materials
Dressmaking pins
Polystyrene glue (tube)
Stanley knife
Ruler
Pencil
Polystyrene board (see art and craft shops)

Method
1. Cut out items from polystyrene board to sizes shown. (*Hint*: Use end of bank as template for other 2.)
2. Cut large piece of polystyrene (top of the bank) 7 cm from end (lengthways) for easier bending into shape of bank. (Do not cut all way through.)
3. Glue and pin all parts together.

top of bank

score with Stanley knife
for bending and glue to edge

51 cm

20 cm

7 cm

7 cm

end of bank

2 cm

18 cm

3.5 cm

51 cm

pin till glue sets

8
Consensiball

JOHN MERINO

Description

This is a physical activity focusing on planning and implementation of a consensus oriented exercise. It helps explore barriers to consensus and the influence of hidden assumptions.

This game can also be used as a warm-up for an experiential learning program when further outdoor activities will follow.

Learning opportunity

- To clarify the meaning of group consensus.
- To show how a group reaches consensus.
- To identify the distractions and negative aspects of group dynamics that can impede progress towards achieving group goals.

Audience

Work groups where people already know each other, or groups of people who have not previously met.

Resources

You'll need:

- 1 ball (such as a soccer ball, volleyball or basketball)
- Video camera to tape the action and replay as part of the debriefing

Setting

Outdoors in a park, field or any open, flat, grassy and safe playing area.

TIME 30–45 min.

30–45 minutes:
- 10 minutes for Round 1
- 5 minutes for Round 2
- 15–30 minutes for the debriefing

GROUP SIZE 6–15

6–15 people. When this game is played with groups of more than 15 people, interactions can be cumbersome, with some group members' involvement diminishing.

Briefing

- Form a large circle with people at least 1 m apart.
- Take 1 minute to practise passing the ball randomly from player to player across the circle.
- Ensure that each participant has practised catching and passing at least once.
- Stop the action and introduce the following statement as the goal:

> Our goal is to agree on how long we can keep the ball off the ground and in the air by consensus; every member of the group must be involved.

Players can use their head, feet and/or legs to keep the ball in the air. The chest can be used to stop or trap the ball, but players must stay roughly in the original circle.

Team members can have multiple attempts at passing on the ball, but should try to pass the ball to other team members as quickly as is practical.

Process

There will be approximately 10 minutes to try out the rules and decide (through group consensus) how long the team can keep the ball off the ground and in the air.

Debriefing

- Stop the action by calling out: 'Your time is up.'
- Use the following questions to explore the experience:
  - Did you achieve the goal of agreeing on the length of time you can keep the ball off the ground and in the air?
  - What were the group processes for achieving the goal?
  - How were the goals communicated among team members?
  - Did you practice/rehearse to gauge the validity of your estimate?
  - What hidden beliefs (about how to play with a ball of the type used) influenced individual/group behaviour?
  - Did anyone recognise that such hidden beliefs existed?
  - Did they attempt to/succeed in changing them?
  - What parallels with 'real life' could be drawn from the process experienced?
- If players seem keen, and there is time, you may allow them the time to see if they can achieve their stated goal.

Circle of safety

SANDRA SHEEHAN

Description

A non-threatening way for group members to share and validate options and knowledge. It also highlights knowledge areas requiring additional attention.

Learning opportunity

- To evaluate learning and changes in attitude, and to encourage group participation.
- To create an environment where participants can experience benefits through differing perspectives.
- Alternatively, this activity can be used to encourage discussion regarding mutual problems/solutions. This activity is particularly useful for quieter members whose participation can otherwise be less active.

Audience

People who have participated in a learning experience and are now reflecting on the learning and/or problems that were encountered.

Resources

You'll need:

- Sufficient question cards—prepared ahead of time—to cover the knowledge area involved in the training session which preceded the activity. Alternatively, participants can write the question cards themselves and the activity can be used as a tool for exploring problems that have arisen
- Container to hold the cards
- Pens
- 1 chair for each participant, plus 1 extra

TIME 60–90 min.

60–90 minutes, depending on the amount of information involved.

GROUP SIZE 10–12

10–12 people.

Setting

An area where chairs can be set in a circle, with enough room for people to stand and move to new seats in the circle.

Briefing

Explain that this is an activity to review understanding and knowledge of the course material. Before commencing, ask the group to decide how to handle any unanswered queries or issues that may be *too hot to handle*. Once this is agreed, explain the process to be used (see below) and then begin the activity once everyone is seated in the circle. Announce that you will keep track of the process and remind everyone when it is time to move to a new chair.

Process

- Participants move their chairs into a circle.
- Place 1 extra chair in the circle.
- Participants take their seats, but leave 1 chair vacant.
- Each participant picks a question card from the lucky draw.
- The person to the left of the vacant chair reads aloud the question on their card. The person on their left suggests an answer to the question. The next person to the left also suggests an answer to the question before the remainder of the group can add additional information.

- Once the question is satisfactorily answered, participants move 1 seat to the right, but leave the original vacant seat empty.
- Again, the person to the left of the vacant chair reads aloud the question on their card. The person on their left suggests an answer to the question and then the next person on the left suggests an answer before the remainder of the group adds additional information.
- The process continues until all participants have discussed the question on their card.

Debriefing

- Ask:
  - How has this activity assisted in team building? (Draw out the benefits of other people's perspectives.)
  - In what ways has this activity generated group consensus?
  - What are the benefits of group ownership of solutions?
- Seek a comment from each participant about how they feel now, along with at least one major learning point.
- Clarify any unresolved issues and an appropriate strategy for dealing with them.
- Reinforce areas that have been highlighted as requiring additional clarification.

10 Bridging the gap

KELLY SCOTT

TIME 40 min.

About 40 minutes:
- 10 minutes for briefing
- 20 minutes for planning and construction
- 10 minutes for debriefing

GROUP SIZE 6–10

A minimum of 6 and a maximum of 10 participants. If you have a larger group you can arrange them in 2 sets of teams in separate parts of a large space and double all your resources requirements.

Description

A teamwork exercise involving physical activity and creativity with emphasis on communication problems.

Learning opportunity

- To demonstrate the importance of communication and problem solving within a team environment.
- To highlight the value of team effort while, at the same time, emphasising that individual performance can also enhance team performance.

Audience

Any group experiencing difficulty in managing relationships, in working as a team or in solving work problems.

Resources

You'll need:

- About 40–60 plastic drinking straws
- 2 containers of sewing/dressmaking pins
- 2 blindfolds
- 2 pieces of soft cloth for use as mouth gags
- 1 roll of masking tape

Note: No writing materials of any kind are to be used by anyone.

Setting

Indoors or outdoors, with at least 3–4 m² of fairly level ground.

Preparation

- Tape 2 parallel lines 1.5 m in length and approximately 1.5 m apart on to the floor. The area between the lines of tape represents a flooded river.
- Divide the participants into 2 teams, with a minimum of 3 per team (equal numbers if possible).
- In each team, identify one person to be blindfolded and another person who will be unable to speak.

Briefing

- Inform the participants that their task is to *build a free-standing bridge across the flooded river to allow communications to be restored.*
- All team members from one team stand on one side of the riverbank and the other team's members stand on the other side of the riverbank.
- Each team is responsible for building half of the bridge, which must be joined by the end of the exercise.

- Ask each team to blindfold 1 team member and use one of the pieces of soft cloth as a mouth gag (or put a small piece of masking tape on their hand) to remind another team member to remain silent throughout the process. Stress that all participants must be actively involved in the building of their half of the bridge.
- Give each team 20–30 drinking straws and 1 container of pins. Explain that these are the only resources they can use to build the bridge in 20 minutes.

Process

- Allow the teams to plan and construct the bridge as they see fit.
- Let them know when they have 5 minutes time remaining.
- When the bridge is nearing completion, you can offer the masking tape to help the teams to 'bridge the gap'.

Debriefing

Ask:

- What were the important factors in getting the bridge built?
- How did communication flow?
- What factors hindered the team and why?
- What individual contributions assisted the teams?
- What would you do differently if you were to do this again?
- What does this exercise tell us about the value of teams?
- To what extent did each team use creative strategies to build the bridge?
- How did each team manage communications between the 2 groups?
- Did a leader (or leaders) emerge?

11 Chaordic construction

JANELL CARTER

Description

A teamwork activity combining a set of simple construction tasks with a more complex requirement to conceptualise a 'whole' item when only part of the whole is known to each team. It represents the type of workplace where components of a whole item are developed at separate sites and then brought together for completion.

Learning opportunity

- To give participants an insight into the types of communication problems that may be encountered in any large organisation.

Audience

People at all levels in organisations, especially those communicating with other sections, departments or others in different locations.

Resources

You'll need:

- 1 drinking straw (at least 16 cm long) for Department 1
- 17 paddlepop sticks (3 paddlepop sticks for Department 2 and 14 for Department 3)
- 1 tape measure or ruler for each work team (if requested)
- 3 pairs of scissors (1 pair each for Departments 1, 4 and 5)
- 1 pen and paper for each work team
- 1 sheet of plastic at least 23 cm x 13 cm for Department 4
- 1 piece of string of at least 90 cm long for Department 4
- 3 sheets of coloured paper (A4 size is fine) for Department 5

TIME 1.25 hours

Approximately 1.25 hours. The simulation is run in 3 stages:
- 20 minutes (approx.) for planning and construction
- 10 minutes (approx.) to bring separate pieces together
- 45 minutes (approx.) for debriefing

GROUP SIZE 10

A minimum of 10 and a maximum of 25 people. The simulation can be adapted to accommodate a larger group by having 2 organisations compete to complete the project first.

- Rolls of masking tape, glue and/or reusable adhesive (e.g. Blu–Tack) to assist with attaching the pieces in Stage 2 and to be given as 'additional resources' if requested in writing in Stage 1
- A completed model of the trailer (made by following the instructions for each department and then combining the separate sections to form a two-wheel box-trailer)

Setting

The simulation can be run indoors or outdoors, but you'll need enough room to allow each work team to plan and construct independently in Stage 1. If possible, each work team should not be within hearing distance of each other. In addition, one large room or area is required for Stages 2 and 3.

Briefing

- Divide the group into 5 work teams of approximately equal size.
- During Stage 1, each work team is to produce a separate part of the larger construct. The pieces will be brought together to complete the project in Stage 2.
- Distribute *Department instruction sheets* and clarify that after each team has completed their construction, they must provide a brief written description of what they perceive the whole construction will look like and how it will be used when it is brought together in Stage 2.
- *Do not* give the teams any clues about the nature of the whole item.
- Have the resources sorted into departments and ready for collection.

Process

- Stand aside and observe as the teams come to grips with their instructions. Answer only basic questions (e.g. 'Where should we do this?'). Do not explain how or why it is to be done.
- Distribute resources when requested. Additional resources must be requested in writing.
- Allow 15–20 minutes for Stage 1 (planning and construction).
- Let teams know when they have only 5 minutes remaining.
- Check that all teams have a written visual outline of what they perceive the whole construction will look like before allowing all work teams to bring pieces together for final construction to complete the object.
- After 10 minutes, ask the group to present to you the finished object for assessment of its viability for sale. This is the end of the game.

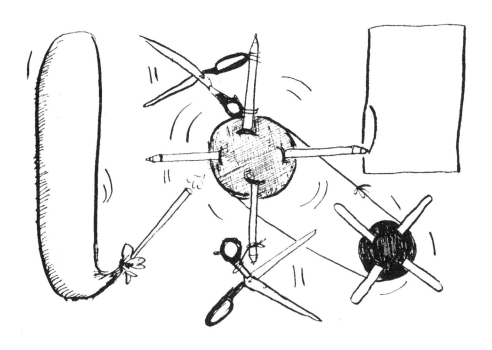

Debriefing

- Have each team read and/or show what they perceived the object to be (keep this light-hearted). If they have not constructed a box trailer, tell them that this was the intended outcome and display the model you have prepared.
- Ask:
  - What happened when you were presented with the original information?
  - How did you feel within your work team doing the set tasks?
  - When the teams came together in Stage 2, what happened to you as an individual and as a team?
  - What would have made the job easier?
  - How does this relate to communication within large organisations?

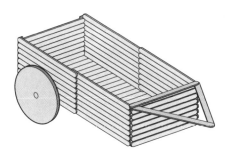

Department 1 instruction sheet

- You are part of a large organisation with departments situated all over the country.
- The organisation is manufacturing equipment, but because of its size, each department will produce only one part of the whole.
- After you've completed your part of the whole, you must write a brief description of what your team believes the whole item will look like and how it will be used.
- Once these requirements are completed, your work team should assist other departments in bringing together all the pieces for Stage 2—which will be announced by the facilitator.

Departmental tasks
- Select a spokesperson to liaise with the General Manager (the facilitator), but you will have to make do with the information that you receive.
- Send your spokesperson to collect the following resources from the General Manager (the facilitator):
  - 1 sheet of cardboard
  - 1 drinking straw
  - Pen and paper
  - 1 pair of scissors
- Within 15–20 minutes you're to construct the following with the materials supplied to you. You may, however, request some additional resources from the General Manager. All such requests must be in writing.

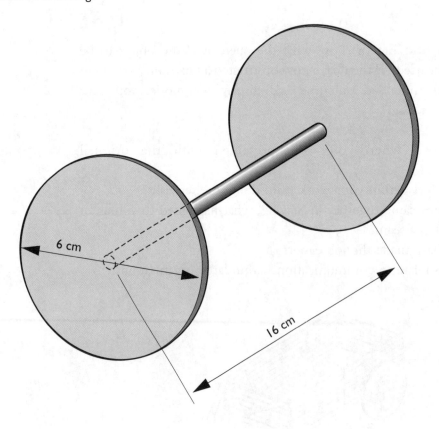

Department 2 instruction sheet

STAGE 1
- You are part of a large organisation with departments situated all over the country.
- The organisation is manufacturing equipment, but because of its size, each department will produce only one part of the whole.
- After you've completed your part of the whole, you must write a brief description of what your team believes the whole item will look like and how it will be used.
- Once these requirements are completed, your work team should assist other departments in bringing together all the pieces for Stage 2—which will be announced by the facilitator.

Departmental tasks
- Select a spokesperson to liaise with the General Manager (the facilitator), but you will have to make do with the information that you receive.
- Send your spokesperson to collect the following resources from the General Manager (the facilitator):
  - 3 paddlepop sticks
  - Pen and paper
- Within 15–20 minutes you're to construct the following with the materials supplied to you. You may, however, request some additional resources from the General Manager. All such requests must be in writing.

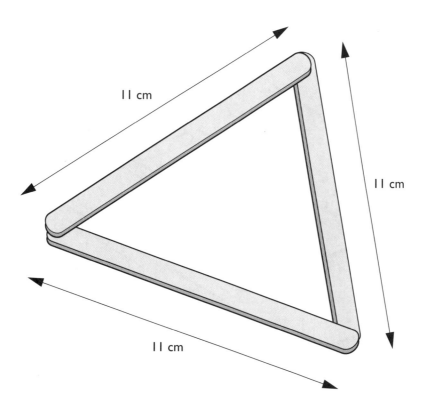

Department 3 instruction sheet

STAGE 1
- You are part of a large organisation with departments situated all over the country.
- The organisation is manufacturing equipment, but because of its size, each department will produce only one part of the whole.
- After you've completed your part of the whole, you must write a brief description of what your team believes the whole item will look like and how it will be used.
- Once these requirements are completed, your work team should assist other departments in bringing together all the pieces for Stage 2—which will be announced by the facilitator.

Departmental tasks
- Select a spokesperson to liaise with the General Manager (the facilitator), but you will have to make do with the information that you receive.
- Send your spokesperson to collect the following resources from the General Manager (the facilitator):
  - 14 paddlepop sticks
  - Pen and paper
- Within 15–20 minutes you're to construct the following with the materials supplied to you. You may, however, request some additional resources from the General Manager. All such requests must be in writing.

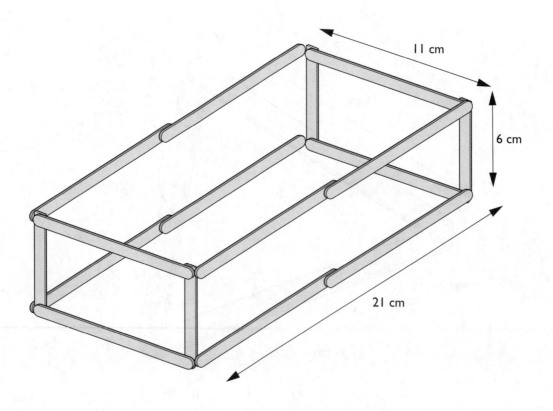

11 cm

6 cm

21 cm

Department 4 instruction sheet

STAGE 1
- You are part of a large organisation with departments situated all over the country.
- The organisation is manufacturing equipment, but because of its size, each department will initially have to produce only a separate part of the whole.
- After you've completed your part of the whole, you must write a brief description of what your team believes the whole item will look like and how it will be used.
- Once these requirements are completed, your work team should assist other departments in bringing together all the pieces for Stage 2—which will be announced by the facilitator.

Departmental tasks
- Select a spokesperson to liaise with the General Manager (the facilitator), but you will have to make do with the information that you receive.
- Send your spokesperson to collect the following resources from the General Manager (the facilitator):
  - 1 length of string (90 cm long)
  - 1 plastic sheet
  - 1 pair of scissors
  - Pen and paper
- Within 15–20 minutes you're to construct the following with the materials supplied to you. You may, however, request some additional resources from the General Manager. All such requests must be in writing.

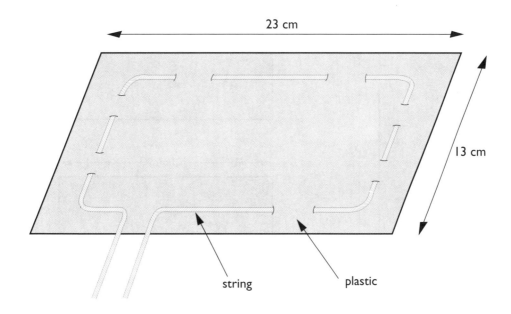

string   plastic

Department 5 instruction sheet

STAGE 1
- You are part of a large organisation with departments situated all over the country.
- The organisation is manufacturing equipment, but because of its size, each department will produce only one part of the whole.
- After you've completed your part of the whole, you must write a brief description of what your team believes the whole item will look like and how it will be used.
- Once these requirements are completed, your work team should assist other departments in bringing together all the pieces for Stage 2—which will be announced by the facilitator.

Departmental tasks
- Select a spokesperson to liaise with the General Manager (the facilitator), but you will have to make do with the information that you receive.
- Send your spokesperson to collect the following resources from the General Manager (the facilitator):
  - 3 sheets of coloured paper
  - 1 pair of scissors
  - Pen and paper
- Within 15–20 minutes you're to construct the following with the materials supplied to you. You may, however, request some additional resources from the General Manager. All such requests must be in writing.
  - 1 x base (21 cm x 11 cm)
  - 2 x sides (11 cm x 6.5 cm)
  - 2 x sides (21 cm x 6.5 cm)

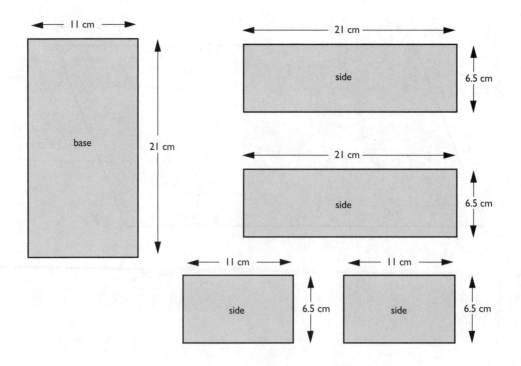

12 Playground

JOANNA HALIORIS

Description

A negotiation exercise involving community priorities, funding decisions, teamwork and decision making.

Learning opportunity

• To identify, assess and negotiate options within and among teams to meet agreement in a structured way.

Audience

People who may be required to resolve conflict, negotiate and liaise with others in team environments.

Resources

You'll need:

• Copies of the 3 instruction sheets (1 for each team) and copies for yourself
• 3 copies of the work sheet
• 10 photocopies of the dollars page to make a total of $8000 cut into denominations of 10 x $500, 20 x $100 and 20 x $50
• Timer (to monitor the timing of each of the 6 steps)
• Copy of the *Prices for playground equipment* for each team

Setting

Indoors or outdoors where 3 teams can develop strategies independently, but come together for negotiation and debriefing.

> **TIME 1.5–2 hours**
>
> A total of approximately 1.5–2 hours:
> • About 1 hour for the action
> • About 30–60 minutes for feedback and debriefing

> **GROUP SIZE 12**
>
> A minimum of 12 and a maximum of 24 people. If there are more than 24, ask the extra people to be observers.

Briefing

- Divide the group into 3 independent teams and tell them they'll be negotiating to construct a playground.
- Explain that the teams' roles and tasks are described on their instruction sheets.
- Distribute the instruction sheets and work sheets.

Process

- Explain that you will allow a few minutes for teams to come to grips with their roles before you announce the start of Step 1.
- Set a timer for 7 minutes and when the time is up, announce the start of Step 1.
- Facilitate the flow through of the remaining steps as follows:

Initial preparation	7 minutes	Coming to grips with team roles and tasks
Step 1	15 minutes	Within each team, generate options for design of playground
Step 2	6 minutes	Inter-team negotiation with other concerned parties (Round 1). Only the team representative can negotiate
Step 3	10 minutes	Within each team, discussion of negotiation outcome and subsequent adjustment of design
Step 4	6 minutes	Inter-team negotiation (Round 2). Only the team representative can negotiate
Step 5	10 minutes	Within each team, last chance for adjustments to design to meet needs of all parties—hopefully to reach agreement
Step 6	6 minutes	Final round of negotiation to reach agreement (or otherwise) among teams' representatives

- Conclude the action and bring all the team members together for the debriefing.

Debriefing

- Ask for feedback on what happened.
- Seek details of creative options for the design from each team.
- Did all team members have an opportunity to contribute?
- Discuss the importance of planning and preparing options for negotiation.
- Discuss the principles of win/lose, lose/lose and win/win negotiation.
- Did teams feel negotiations were based on a win/win philosophy?
- Discuss the value of a structured approach to problem solving, resolving conflict and negotiation.

Instruction sheet for council representatives

Background

Your group represents the council, which has granted a budget of $8000 to be spent as your team sees fit on building a children's playground in your local area. All funding must be disbursed in this financial year. If mutually acceptable agreements cannot be negotiated, the grant will be suspended indefinitely.

Task

You're preparing your ideas and/or design for the playground. You're to seek input from the local community as well as from the local building company that won the tender, Playsafe Constructions Pty Ltd. You must keep in mind the building regulations and environmental regulations, as well as the issues of playground maintenance and safety and the ever-present threat of vandalism.

Rules

- Nominate a member of your team to:
  - meet with a representative from the local community;
  - meet with Playsafe Constructions Pty Ltd;
  - collect funding of $8000 (via the game facilitator), which will be supplied in cash denominations of 10 x $500, 20 x $100 and 20 x $50.
- For every $100 spent on equipment, an additional $100 must be spent on wages to erect the equipment.
- For every $500 spent on materials and/or equipment, a minimum of an additional $100 must be spent to ensure minimum safety and minimum environmental regulations are adhered to.
- Allow time for the remaining steps as follows:

Initial preparation	7 minutes	Coming to grips with team roles and tasks
Step 1	15 minutes	Within each team, generate options for design of playground
Step 2	6 minutes	Inter-team negotiation with other concerned parties (Round 1). Only the team representative can negotiate
Step 3	10 minutes	Within each team, discussion of negotiation outcome and subsequent adjustment of design
Step 4	6 minutes	Inter-team negotiation (Round 2). Only the team representative can negotiate
Step 5	10 minutes	Within each team, last chance for adjustments to design to meet needs of all parties—hopefully to reach agreement
Step 6	6 minutes	Final round of negotiation to reach agreement (or otherwise) among teams' representatives

Instruction sheet for Playsafe Constructions Pty Ltd

Background

You are Playsafe Constructions Pty Ltd. You have won the tender to build a children's playground in your local area. The council has granted a total budget of $8000 for the playground. Although you're well known and respected within the community, in order to win the contract the Playsafe Constructions Pty Ltd quote included a very small profit margin. Your sales figures have recently been worryingly low. You've heard through the grapevine that the council plans to construct other sites in the near future, so you want to build something that is fun for the children and looks good for future public relations purposes. You are privy to a newly available colourful equipment line of products that looks really inviting to children and is not labour intensive to construct or maintain.

Task

You're preparing your ideas and/or design for the playground.

Rules

- Nominate a member of your team to:
  - meet with a representative from the council;
  - meet with a representative from the local community;
  - collect funding (via the council representative), which will be supplied in cash denominations of 10 x $500, 20 x $100 and 20 x $50.
- For every $100 paid to you for equipment, an additional $100 must be spent on wages to erect the equipment.
- For every $500 paid to you on materials and/or equipment, a minimum of an additional $100 must be spent to ensure minimum safety and minimum environmental regulations are adhered to.
- Allow time for the remaining steps as follows:

Initial preparation	7 minutes	Coming to grips with team roles and tasks
Step 1	15 minutes	Within each team, generate options for design of playground
Step 2	6 minutes	Inter-team negotiation with other concerned parties (Round 1). Only the team representative can negotiate
Step 3	10 minutes	Within each team, discussion of negotiation outcome and subsequent adjustment of design
Step 4	6 minutes	Inter-team negotiation (Round 2). Only the team representative can negotiate
Step 5	10 minutes	Within each team, last chance for adjustments to design to meet needs of all parties—hopefully to reach agreement
Step 6	6 minutes	Final round of negotiation to reach agreement (or otherwise) among teams' representatives

Instruction sheet for community representatives

Background

Your group consists of well known and respected members of the community. The local council has granted a total budget of $8000 for the construction of a children's playground in your local area. As members of the community, you're concerned about the health and safety of the children and parents as well as the environment. You're not only looking for equipment that's safe, but also fun and inviting. The government's recent skin cancer warnings have alerted you to issues of protection by trees. Shading is a high priority for you. Playground equipment varies in price. A swing can be a simple construction made from iron with chains or it can have rubber and extra stabilisation for toddlers.

Task

You're preparing your ideas and/or design for the playground.

Rules

- Nominate a member of your team to meet with a representative from the council and a Playsafe Constructions Pty Ltd representative.
- Oversee the distribution of funding, which will be supplied in cash denominations of 10 x $500, 20 x $100 and 20 x $50.
- For every $100 paid to you for equipment, an additional $100 must be spent on wages to erect the equipment.
- For every $500 paid to you on materials and/or equipment, a minimum of an additional $100 must be spent to ensure minimum safety and minimum environmental regulations are adhered to.
- Allow time for the remaining steps as follows:

Initial preparation	7 minutes	Coming to grips with team roles and tasks
Step 1	15 minutes	Within each team, generate options for design of playground
Step 2	6 minutes	Inter-team negotiation with other concerned parties (Round 1). Only the team representative can negotiate
Step 3	10 minutes	Within each team, discussion of negotiation outcome and subsequent adjustment of design
Step 4	6 minutes	Inter-team negotiation (Round 2). Only the team representative can negotiate
Step 5	10 minutes	Within each team, last chance for adjustments to design to meet needs of all parties—hopefully to reach agreement
Step 6	6 minutes	Final round of negotiation to reach agreement (or otherwise) among teams' representatives

Work sheet

Equipment	Materials
Wages	**Safety**
Environment	**Maintenance**

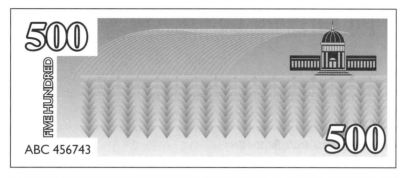

500
FIVE HUNDRED
500
ABC 456743

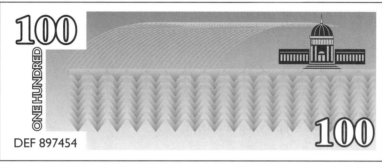

100
ONE HUNDRED
100
DEF 897454

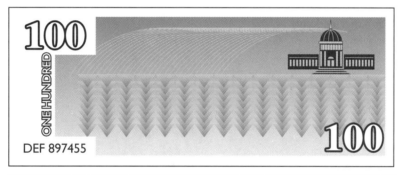

100
ONE HUNDRED
100
DEF 897455

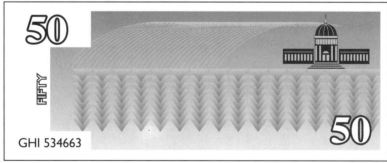

50
FIFTY
50
GHI 534663

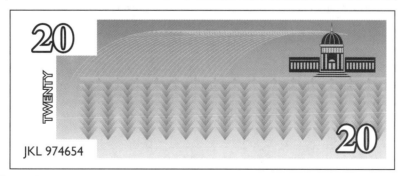

20
TWENTY
20
JKL 974654

Prices for playground equipment

Swings

Coloured metal bars and timber seat for children 5 years and over

• Single swing	$250
• Double swing	$450

Coloured metal bars and safety seats for toddlers

• Single swing	$250
• Double swing	$450

Aluminium bars with chains and rubber seat

• Single swing	$150
• Double swing	$250

Slippery dip

• Plain slippery dip with steps	$400
• Monkey bar coloured with slippery dip and steps	$650

Seesaw

• With handle at either end only	$400
• With seats for safety	$500

Cubbyhouse

• Small—timber logs	$400
• Large—timber logs	$600

Park bench

• Coloured metal	$250
• Timber on metal frame	$400
• Timber log bench (no back support)	$150

Rubber tiles for playground area, per tile (50 x 50 cm)	$15
Shading over central playground area	$1000
Bark, shrubs and trees to be negotiated	

No item is compulsory, other items could be introduced and everything is subject to negotiation.

13 RiftRaft Inc.

ELYSSEBETH LEIGH AND DON CHANTLER

Description

A team-based activity, replicating issues which arise when people are asked to negotiate from a values base. Participants adopt distinctive roles with quite different values and needs, but they must achieve agreement about the outcomes or miss out on funding for the task they all want to achieve. The activity provides practice in developing awareness of differences in perceptions and expectations and the steps required to achieve negotiated agreements.

Learning opportunity

- To develop awareness about different perceptions of learning needs that can be held by members of different groups. All the people are involved in the one situation, and must consider ways in which their different perceptions can be rationalised and combined into a program to meet the needs and expectations of all those involved.

Audience

People involved in making decisions about training and development strategies.

Resources

You'll need:

- Chairs for participants (and tables if participants need them)
- Writing materials
- 3 flip chart stands and paper (optional)
- Copies of the *Press release* and the appropriate briefing sheet for each team

TIME   **1 hour**

An absolute minimum of 60 minutes.

GROUP SIZE 9–15

Between 9 and 15 participants arranged in 3 teams. More than 15 participants: allocate them to further teams in such a way that you continue to have sub-sets of 3 groups (numbers within each sub-set may differ without causing problems).

Setting

A flat-floored room with sufficient space to allow each sub-set to develop their strategies out of hearing of the others. There must be room for groups to work comfortably in their own area and also have representatives move to a 'neutral' space for negotiation meetings. If you are able to provide separate rooms for each group, it is still necessary to have a room large enough to fit the total group. Conduct all the briefing and debriefing in the large room.

Briefing

- Explain the objectives and scenario (i.e. groups of people involved in making plans/decisions about an innovative learning program).
- Allocate participants in approximately equal numbers to small groups and arrange them in their separate spaces.
- Tell groups their roles (i.e. 'learners'; accredited 'education providers' or RiftRaft Inc. 'managers').
- Distribute the *Press release* and *General briefing* sheet and allow 5 minutes for reading.
- Invite questions (but avoid giving information that may pre-empt later group decisions).

- Distribute specific briefing sheets. Groups receive their own set of information only.
- Announce that: 'Each group is to develop a set of strategic statements outlining their needs for an education program to fit the situation described in the information provided. Each group is to nominate 1 representative for a meeting to be held in approximately 15 minutes.'

Process

- After the initial 15 minutes (during which groups develop the outlines of their particular needs), the group representatives meet in the larger negotiation space for a briefing meeting of about 10 minutes. During the briefing meeting, representatives state their stances and expectations. Others may listen, but no decisions are made at this time.
- Representatives return to their own areas to prepare a negotiating position for a second meeting (again in approximately 15 minutes time). Groups may appoint a second representative for this second meeting.
- Representative/s return to the negotiating meeting to state and then discuss their positions (about 15 minutes). Their goal is to develop a joint position for attracting external funds to develop the agreed program. No agreement = no funds!

Debriefing

Ask such questions as:

- What happened at each stage?
- How were people feeling?
- Did groups change their position to ensure agreement? How did they change? Why these changes?
- Were there winners and/or losers and, if so, who and why?
- What are parallels with real-life situations?
- What issues about workplace learning were illuminated by the various discussions?

Press release

RiftRaft Inc.

New opportunities for employment and rural economy

I have recently returned from the outback as a guest of RiftRaft Inc. for trials of its wonder product RiftRaft.

The company has announced that extensive development will take place in a number of isolated rural centres in all states across Australia. Production plans are to be backed with a multimillion dollar budget. A large proportion of this budget is earmarked for development and presentation of learning programs. It is anticipated that these programs will attract funding from government authorities charged with the development of new industries in rural and remote areas.

RiftRaft has enormous potential both at home and as a major export dollar earner. The production methods require clean air, free of carbon monoxide and sulfur, thus prohibiting development of facilities near existing urban industrial areas. The technology involved is relatively low cost but quite complex in its implementation, hence the early emphasis on the development of appropriate learning strategies. The skills required in the process are unlike any others in our current workforce. Each employee needs to acquire a range of skills to ensure continuity of production because of the small numbers of employees in each plant.

My experience of RiftRaft was enough to make me an instant convert. Everyone who has had contact with it expresses the same degree of enthusiasm for the concept.

Congratulations to RiftRaft Inc. on its innovative approach to boosting rural industry.

Construction of facilities at many centres is well advanced. Production is expected to begin as soon as there are enough trained staff available. RiftRaft Inc. has begun employing residents in surrounding towns and will shortly convene meetings to consider the best approaches to developing the learning programs.

Keep your eyes open. There's excitement ahead!

RiftRaft Inc.: General briefing

In the development of any educational program at least 3 groups of people are involved:

- the organisation/employing body
- the educators
- the learners

Each of these groups has, or could have, an input into the planning and development of the learning program.

During this activity, you'll be a member of one group. The group's task is to identify your major areas of concern and interest regarding the shape, form and direction of a specific learning/education program, when considered from the perspective of the group you represent.

Phase 1

In the next 15 minutes please:

- agree on a list of factors that you all regard as essential to a successful program under the circumstances described;
- identify a group representative to present your list at the first joint committee of representatives from groups of educators, learners and RiftRaft Inc.

Phase 2

This is the first of 2 meetings of the joint committee.

- During this phase, representatives introduce themselves and have 2 minutes to present their group's list of essential factors.
- This 10 minute meeting is simply to inform each other about the items that need to be included in the learning/education program.
- No negotiations are allowed at this stage, but other group members may listen to the presentations and note the requirements of the other groups.

Phase 3

Groups reconvene in their own areas and review their objectives in the light of what has been said, then prepare for another meeting of the committee.

- Approximately 15 minutes are allowed for this part of the process.
- Groups can appoint a second representative to speak at the next meeting.

Phase 4

The joint committee meets a second time to finalise the process to be developed.

- Representatives state their positions and *negotiate* for consensus on a learning program strategy to meet the priorities of all groups.
- *No agreement = no external funds!*

Briefing: Educators

You are a group of educators from an accredited education provider and have been asked to design a learning program for employees of RiftRaft Inc.

The production processes involved are complex and unique to the product. Tasks can be performed by 'average' workers with appropriate learning. The program must provide for both practical and theoretical learning in all aspects of the production process.

You are acknowledged providers of top quality programs. As members of a registered training organisation (RTO), *you believe it's important to retain control of the direction and focus of this new program.* You want to develop a program to your usual high standards, which can be accredited nationally. You know that the company has invited input from its new employees and its senior management team. You will meet them shortly to compare ideas.

Briefing: RiftRaft company representatives

You are members of a management team from RiftRaft Inc.

You've been asked to advise on the requirements for a learning program to bring production on-line in the shortest possible time.

It is company policy to recruit from the local community. New employees must be able to handle all the new processes and concepts involved.

You're to develop guidelines for an acceptable learning program to provide on-time commencement of production. You know that *any delays beyond 3 months of completion of the production facilities will cause major problems.*

The company has requested input from new employees and accredited learning providers. You will meet them shortly to compare ideas.

Briefing: Learners

You are a group of new employees of the company RiftRaft Inc.

You have been asked by RiftRaft to present ideas on training and development for yourselves. Your employer has a policy of recruiting its workforce locally and providing training in the skills and processes involved. Each of you lives in a different remote rural community and you've been brought together for this meeting. Your towns support small primary schools with all post-primary facilities some distance away.

It's understood that salary increments are directly linked to skills acquisition. *You are naturally anxious to develop your skills (and therefore your income) as quickly and effectively as possible.*

A group of educators and a senior management team from the company are also working on this project. You will meet with them shortly.

14 Personal learning outcomes— tropical style!

JEFF KINDER

Description

A short introductory exercise to help participants identify their personal goals for a learning program. It encourages everyone to identify their own goals while listening closely to everyone else, and develop shared lists of goals that can be addressed during the program.

TIME 15 min.
Approximately 15 minutes, depending on the size of the group.

Learning opportunity

• To identify goals that individuals and teams decide to achieve during a learning program.

GROUP SIZE 3–15
3–15 people.

Audience

This exercise can be used early on the first day of longer programs. It assists participants to build rapport with one another and promotes team building.

Resources

You'll need:

• 3 flip chart sheets attached to the wall and prepared with the following headings:

1. Hibiscus
Why are you studying this course?
2. Frangipani
What outcomes do you want to achieve?
3. Orchid
What criteria will you use to measure your success (i.e. how will you know when you have achieved the learning outcomes from this course)?

• A cassette or CD player with tropical balmy, relaxing music
• Chairs set to resemble aircraft seating

Setting

Any room with space to arrange chairs in 2 rows in the centre of the room, and enough room for people to stand at, and write on, 3 widely separated flip chart stands.

Preparation

• Preset chairs, flip charts and music.

Briefing

• Ask participants to stand up, ask them to listen carefully to you, following your instructions as you read them out, and to imagine the scene as you make the following announcement:

This is a message from your pilot(s), captain(s) [use the names of the key staff to be involved in the program]. This training course is being held on a beautiful, tropical Australian island on the Great Barrier Reef where barriers to learning disappear. Welcome to Flight [use the formal name of the learning program where you are using this activity].

Please take your seats on the aircraft for the short flight to the island. Once you all are seated, please turn around and shake hands with the person behind you. [Of course they cannot do this, because the person behind them has also turned around. This produces some confusion and humour as people look to you for help. Smile and acknowledge their confusion without verbal comment.] Buckle your seat belts. Training creates a safety zone where you as learners can try new things—step out of your comfort zones in a risk-free environment.

Now, please settle into your seats and close your eyes. [Pause briefly before moving into the next announcement. Begin this announcement as if you are making a safety announcement in an aircraft.]

We are on the tarmac to begin a learning journey together. This is Flight [use the formal name of the

learning program where you are using this activity]. We are beginning a relaxing, well deserved, first class trip to a beautiful, tropical Australian island on the Great Barrier Reef where barriers to learning disappear. [Pause] Now we have taken off on the journey and are approaching our destination. As our flight is nearing the island, you are preparing yourself to learn many new things and you're opening your mind to new experiences. Think about where you are going on this flight and why you're on this plane. Consider what you're going to get from this trip that you are going to bring home with you. [Allow a moment or two for consideration.] We're now arriving at the airport, disembarking from the plane and, as we feel the warm balmy breezes, we are met by a local welcoming party. They're offering you welcome leis made of beautiful flowers, but you have to choose which one you want. Here are the choices:

• Hibiscus lei (picture the beautiful colours)
• Frangipani lei (smell the perfume)
• Tropical orchid lei (admire the wonderful shapes)
• A mystery choice

Process

Who chose the mystery choice?	Ask these people to wait where they are for a moment.
Who chose the hibiscus? Who chose the frangipani? Who chose the orchid?	Ask people to notice the flip charts with headings and point to where the hibiscus, frangipani and tropical orchid flip charts hang, and to group at the flip charts with others who chose the same flower.

- Tell those who chose the mystery prize that they've won a free SCUBA diving trip to the shark feeding frenzy, and send them to smaller groups to balance the numbers.
- Once everyone is at their place, allow a minute for them to read their group's question on the flip chart. Announce that they're about to hear a piece of music. While the music is playing, they must use the marker pen to write as many short answers as they can to the question on the flip chart sheet in front of them.
- When the music stops, each group is to take its pen and move around the room clockwise to the next flip chart and repeat the process for the new question. Again when the music stops they are to move to the third, and final, flip chart and add responses as before.
- Check that everyone understands, allow time to read the first question and then turn on the music. Play the music and allow the groups to complete each task. Stop the music while they move to the next chart.

Debriefing

- Would some of you share some of the points you noted on any of the sheets?
- What steps do you think may be needed to take us there?
- How will you feel going through each step?
- How are you likely to feel when you've achieved this goal?
- When we began we asked you to turn round and shake hands with the person behind you. This was not really possible because of the very nature of the task—and you were not yet ready. Now that you have had time to build all these lists do you feel more like a team with shared objectives?

Allow time for everyone to contribute to the feedback.

15 Mars huts

PIA CHRISTENSEN

TIME **2 hours**

A total of about 120 minutes:
- 10–15 minutes to brief the game
- 45–50 minutes (approx.) for the action
- Up to 60 minutes for debriefing

GROUP SIZE **6+**

A minimum of 6 and an approximate maximum of 25 participants who form companies (each of 3–5 people).

Description

A competitive activity that focuses on the importance of establishing a clear understanding of the customer's needs.

Learning opportunity

- To identify and improve trainees' abilities to provide effective customer/client service through acknowledging achievements and identifying gaps in attaining overall customer service course objectives.
- The game also taps into trainees' creativity, competitiveness, co-operation and sense of fun.

Audience

Participants in customer service skills courses.

Resources

You'll need:

- Someone to act as 'the customer' who is not known by (or not familiar to) the participants. The 'customer' stays outside the training area during the activity but joins in the debriefing
- Instruction sheet for the customer
- Copies of the *Company handout* (1 per participant)
- *Mars Hut assembly: Basic instructions* (1 set per company)
- Coloured A4 paper
- Coloured pencils or felt pens (1 set per company)
- Scissors (1 per company)
- Flip chart or butcher's paper (l sheet per company) or 6 white A3 sheets
- Selection of pens, pins, sticky tape, reusable adhesive (e.g. Blu-Tack), drinking straws, staplers and rulers (some companies will be very creative!)

Setting

A training area (indoors or outdoors) where teams can work independently and liaise with the *customer*, who is located well away from all the groups.

Briefing

- Introduce the game as a competitive activity which provides opportunities for a lot of fun and learning. Introduce 'the customer' and position them outside the training area with a copy of the *Customer's instructions* to read.
- Divide the whole group into competitive companies (groups of 3–5 participants).
- Distribute the *Company handout*. Let the participants know that more resources will follow, but allow a minute or 2 for reading.
- Announce the aims of the activity by paraphrasing the *Company handout*.
- Allocate all remaining resources, including the instructions for the *Mars hut assembly* process.
- Remind everyone that all appointments with the customer (who is waiting anxiously) must be arranged through the customer's secretary (i.e. you) and that you will remain available for appointments to be made.

Process

- Encourage the *companies* to focus on the requirements of the *Company handout* and stand back to await developments.
- If there appears to be little inclination to see the customer, you may announce from time to time that there are 'plenty of appointment times available and that you would be delighted to make an appointment, should anyone wish to see the customer'.

Trainer's background information

The connection between the *Mars hut assembly: Basic instructions* and the *Company handout* is intentionally unclear, because one of the learning outcomes is for participants to demonstrate their ability to find out, and achieve clarity, about the customer's needs. The sooner the company representatives meet with the customer, the sooner they have the opportunity of realising the customer's requirements. The customer's needs will usually be ascertained only if the company representatives use open questions, active listening and pick up on the customer's body language. It is rare that a company is completely successful in meeting all the requirements of the customer.

Debriefing

Debriefing is critical for allowing *all* participants to vent their feelings. Following an initial round of letting everyone speak, specific customer service issues can be discussed.

- What did you do (what steps were taken) to complete the exercise?
- What selling techniques did you use to win the contract?
- What 'suggestive selling' techniques (if any) did you use during the exercise?
- What problems did you encounter during the exercise? What did you do about them?
- How did you ensure that you met the customer's needs?
- What kinds of questions did you put to the customer?
- What impressions did you get from the customer about your chances of winning the contract and why? (Ask them to report what the customer said, and describe facial expressions and/or body language.)
- What have you learnt from this exercise?
- What would you do differently next time?

Invite additional comments from the customer.

Customer's instructions

- You work for IGSA (Inter-Galactic Systems Authority) and have been assigned the role of selecting a company to produce Mars huts with special criteria.
- You must not purchase any Mars hut that does not meet all of the following criteria. The Mars hut you buy must have:
  - Emergency flotation to assist when landing
  - Gravity deck
  - Oxygen tanks for all occupants, including 1 dog
  - IGSA logo displayed clearly
  - 2 egresses (1 normal passage out and 1 emergency exit)
- And it must be:
  - At least 2 colours
  - Able to sleep 4
  - Easy to assemble (the Mars surface will not hold pegs in place)
  - Light and easy to store in a small compartment on the spacecraft

Important

- *Please don't give any information that isn't requested* (e.g. you may be asked 'What do you want?', to which you would answer: 'A hut, which I can use on Mars.'). You wouldn't expand on your answer. If asked: 'What does IGSA stand for?', answer: 'Inter-Galactic Systems Authority', but don't expand to say that you'd really like it displayed on the Mars hut.
- Answer 'yes' or 'no' whenever you can (i.e. it is quite reasonable to do so).
- If asked a question that elicits a comprehensive response (e.g. 'What . . .?' 'How . . .?' 'When . . .?' and 'Where . . .?'), do give a complete answer on that subject.
- Be more willing to give information to people who are friendlier, more concerned and/or willing to meet your needs.
- Each group is allowed to see you for only 5 minutes at a time, by prior appointment.

Company handout

- This is a competitive game.
- Each group is to form a company, with a structure, but you decide the structure and the roles each of you take within the company.
- Each company is in competition with all other companies to produce Mars huts (see separate *Mars hut assembly: Basic instructions*).
- You need to win the contract to produce your Mars huts from the customer.
- To make appointments with the customer, you need to see the secretary (the person directing this activity).
- You may make appointments at any time to see the customer, but each appointment must be a maximum of 5 minutes only: you cannot arrange for 2 appointments to be consecutive (giving you more than 5 minutes with the customer).

Notes

_____

_____

_____

_____

_____

_____

_____

Mars hut assembly: Basic instructions

- Cut a coloured sheet of paper to form a large square.
- Form a triangle, then crease along the imaginary dotted lines (see the diagram right). Fold the right section *in front* so the point rests at the bottom of the left crease. Fold the left section *behind* so the point rests at the bottom of the right crease, but on the far side.

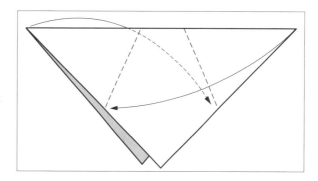

- It should now look approximately like this:

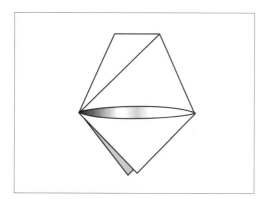

- Fold the indicated point out and up so that it slides into the space between layers.

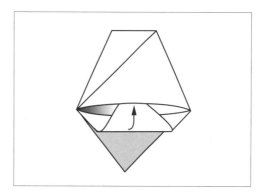

- Turn the Mars hut over and fold the remaining point out and up so that it slides into the space between layers.

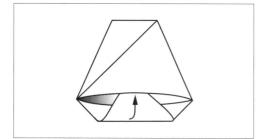

- Your basic Mars hut should now look approximately like this:

Congratulations!

16

Any noise annoys an oyster

LYN ALDERMAN

Description

A quartet of communication skills based activities arranged in a circuit format. Each one has both a competitive and a fun focus.

Learning opportunity

- To share information about communication (particularly emotions and feelings; body language; specific and open questioning techniques).

Audience

Any group of people who are studying communication skills.

Resources

You'll need to organise the following:

- Arrange tables and chairs to form 4 distinct groups marked Table A, Table B, Table C and Table D.
- Label 1 chair per group with the title of 'main role'. The label should be under the seat of the chair so as not to be immediately visible, and is best put on chairs in different places at each table.
- Supply pen and score card for each participant.
- At each table clearly display the rules for the appropriate game.
- Supply Table C with drawing paper.
- Supply Table D with a stack of separate stick-on labels (enough for at least 1 for each player).
- Have some small prizes on hand.

TIME ~2 hours

From 1 hour and 40 minutes to 2 hours. Allow:

- 10 minutes for briefing and for groups to familiarise themselves with the rules of the first game
- 80 minutes for the actual game (4 x 15 minutes for competition, plus 4 x 5 minutes to familiarise themselves with each activity)
- 10–30 minutes for debriefing

GROUP SIZE 12+

A maximum of 36 people. From 12–28 people in 4 groups, with a minimum of 3 and a maximum of 7 per group. For a group of more than 28 people, add a maximum of 2 observers per group.

Setting

A place where 4 groups can make a bit of a commotion without disturbing others in the vicinity.

Briefing

- Ask everyone to gather around you and invite them to join as one of the games athletes to attempt different forms of communication in fun ways at the Communicatolympics. They will have an opportunity to share information and discuss aspects of communication.
- Explain that it may become a little frantic and that *any noise annoys an oyster, but a noisy noise annoys an oyster most.* Non-participants and/or late-comers act as observers.
- There are 4 activities:
  - Table A: *BL Charades*, where a situation is acted out in mime using Body Language;
  - Table B: *Trivia OQ Pursuit*, where Open Questions elicit extensive information;
  - Table C: *PictionEmy*, where EMotions or feelings are depicted graphically on paper; and
  - Table D: *Celebrity SQ Heads*, where Specific Questions elicit specific information.
- Divide the participants into 4 groups and allocate Group 1 to Table A, Group 2 to Table B, Group 3 to Table C and Group 4 to Table D. Explain that each group will start with that table, and then will rotate through the tables to compete in all the activities. Group 1 moves on to Tables B and C, and ends at D. Group 2 moves on to Tables C and D, and ends at A. Group 3 moves on to Tables D and A, and ends at B. Group 4 moves on to Tables A and B, and ends at C.
- Explain that games athletes keep records of their own scores on score cards at the tables using an honour system, which means that the game is self-scoring and honesty is expected. There is 5 minutes after each 15 minute quarter for any extra scoring and record keeping.
- During these 5 minutes, participants are also expected to change activities and become familiar with the new rules.
- As a team, you should ensure that all games athletes are clear on the point score system before starting.
- Points accumulated will depend on how many rounds each team can complete by the end of the 15 minute quarter.
- There are prizes awarded for the funniest Body Language in *BL Charades*

and for the Open Question that draws out the most trivia in *Trivia OQ Pursuit*; an Emy award for the most emotive drawing in *PictionEmy*; and a special prize for the highest score. In *Celebrity SQ Heads*, there is a booby prize for the person voted as needing to ask the most Specific Questions before guessing the identity of the celebrity.

Process

- The facilitator or an observer is the timekeeper and signals the start of each new section.
- Allow 10 minutes for briefing and for groups to familiarise themselves with the rules of the first game, 80 minutes for the actual game (4 x 15 minutes for competition, plus 4 x 5 minutes to familiarise themselves with each activity) and 10–30 minutes for debriefing. Let the games begin!

Debriefing

- The debriefing begins with teams still seated in their last activity. Allow a little time for winding-down discussion. Ask how they enjoyed the games. Did everyone work out what BL, OQ, SQ and PictionEmy refer to? Was there a game that any group enjoyed more than another and, if so, why? How quickly did games athletes form effective teams?
- Now ask members to mingle with games athletes from other teams for a few minutes. Did anyone experience communication difficulties? Were rules interpreted differently?
- Ask for feedback from observers and allocate prizes.
- Next, lead a whole group discussion on various aspects of communication.
  - Is it possible for people to understand each other through body language?
  - What role do feelings and emotions play in communication?
  - Can they help or hinder understandings?
  - When would we want to ask specific questions (e.g. when conversation is becoming sidetracked and we wish to funnel the chat to seek specific, required information)?
  - When would we want to ask open questions to elicit more information? (Perhaps when we need to explore underlying concerns.)
  - What happens when more than one person tries to answer a question?
  - How does this affect communication?
- You may also like to ask the group if the game measured up to its name. Was it a centre of noisy activity?

BL Charades

Aim

The aim is to guess an activity acted out in mime using *body language*. The mimer is the games athlete sitting on the chair that has 'main role' marked under the seat.

Rules

- The mimer writes a scene or situation (e.g. taking out the garbage) on the reverse side of his or her score card.
- The mimer may act only (i.e. no words or sounds are allowed).
- Games athletes guess what the scene or situation is, and call out their answers.
- The mimer judges the correct answers.
- At the end of each round (i.e. when a guess is correct), games athletes change chairs so that a new player is on the 'main role' seat.
- At the end of the 15 minute quarter, Group 1 moves to Table B, Group 2 to Table C, etc.

Scoring

- 1 point for joining the activity
- 5 points for correctly guessing a scene or situation
- 10 points each time you take the 'main role' of mimer
- 1 point for moving to a new seat between rounds
- Bonus 5 points if you have just come from another activity
- Bonus 5 points if this is your fourth activity

Trivia OQ Pursuit

Aim

The aim is to draw out informative answers to *open questions* in the pursuit of trivia. Open questions *don't* invite one word, short or specific answers, but rather more delving replies. (Example of an open question: 'What were your reasons for feeling good the last few times you really laughed aloud?')

Rules

- The question asker, who is the games athlete sitting on the chair labelled 'main role' under the seat, attempts to ask 3 open questions that seek expansive responses.
- The group is to check that the question is indeed a type that promotes open answers rather than one word or short responses.
- At the end of each round (i.e. when 3 open questions have been asked), players change chairs so that a new player is on the 'main role' seat.
- At the end of the 15 minute quarter, move on to your next designated table.

Scoring

- 1 point for joining the activity
- 5 points for responding to a question
- 10 points each time you take the main role of question asker
- 1 point for moving to a new seat between rounds
- Bonus 5 points if you have just come from another activity
- Bonus 5 points if this is your fourth activity

PictionEmy

Aim

The aim is to guess an emotion or feeling from a drawing.

Rules

- The drawer is the games athlete sitting on the chair that has 'main role' marked under the seat.
- The drawer secretly writes a word that represents an emotion or feeling on the reverse side of his or her score card from the following list of choices:

elation	excitement	happiness	affection	empathy	zeal
passion	desire	enthusiasm	impression	tolerance	experience
frustration	endurance	sufferance	sympathy	agitation	sadness
fear	anger	depression	envy	anxiety	fury
despair	pain	terror	agony		

- The drawer attempts to illustrate the emotion or feeling on the supplied drawing paper. Signs and symbols as well as facial expressions and gestures that comment on the picture can be used.
- Games athletes call out their guesses and the first person to answer correctly is the winner. The drawer turns over the card to show that the correct answer matches.
- At the end of each round (i.e. when an emotion or feeling is correctly guessed), players change chairs so that a new player is on the 'main role' seat.
- At the end of the 15 minute quarter, move on to your next designated table.

Scoring

- 1 point for joining the activity
- 5 points for correctly guessing a drawing
- 10 points each time you take the main role of drawer
- 1 point for moving to a new seat between rounds
- Bonus 5 points if you have just come from another activity
- Bonus 5 points if this is your fourth activity

Celebrity SQ Heads

Aim
The aim is to guess the name of the celebrity by asking specific questions. A specific question requires short answers (e.g. 'How tall am I?' or 'What is the colour of my hair?').

Rules
- All games athletes write 1 commonly known, famous name on each of 2 stick-on labels and place the labels face down in the centre of the table. One games athlete picks a label randomly from the centre pile and sticks it on the celebrity's forehead without the celebrity seeing or hearing the identity. The celebrity is the games athlete sitting on the chair that has 'main role' marked under the seat.
- The celebrity attempts to ask specific questions in order to find out his or her identity.
- Games athletes are to reply with one word or short, specific answers only.
- At the end of each round (i.e. when the celebrity has correctly guessed his or her identity), games athletes change chairs so that a new player is on the 'main role' seat.
- At the end of the 15 minute quarter, move on to your next designated table.

Scoring
- 1 point for joining the activity
- 5 points for responding to a question
- 10 points each time you take the main role of celebrity
- 1 point for moving to a new seat between rounds
- Bonus 5 points if you have just come from another activity
- Bonus 5 points if this is your fourth activity

Score card

I am in group _____

We began at table _____

My scores were:

- BL Charades: _____

- Trivia OQ Pursuit: _____

- PictionEmy: _____

- Celebrity SQ Heads: _____

Total: _____

Team total: _____

Working space for calculating scores:

17

Territorial terrain

JEFF KINDER

TIME I hour

A minimum of 60 minutes:
- Briefing: 10 minutes
- Reading: 5 minutes
- Round 1: 5 minutes
- Round 2: 10 minutes
- Round 3: 5 minutes
- Round 4: 10 minutes
- Debriefing: 15 minutes

GROUP SIZE 25

A maximum of 25 participants (i.e. 5 teams of 5). Extra people can act as observers. Smaller numbers can be accommodated by having fewer teams with fewer people in each team, but you would need a minimum of 2 teams of 3 people.

Description

A team-based activity, which brings out the problems of negotiating in what appears to be a competitive environment.

Learning opportunity

- To practise negotiation techniques and strategies that lead to win/win negotiation outcomes for teams.

Audience

Any group of people who have received (or are about to receive) some training in negotiation techniques and strategies.

Resources

You'll need:

- 1 sheet of paper and pens for each team
- Several metres of different coloured streamers or ribbon for each team
- Sticky/masking tape (strong enough to stick the streamers or ribbon to the carpet/ground and or other obstacles, trees and/or furniture, depending on whether you're running the simulation indoors or outdoors)
- 1 pair of scissors for each team
- 1 copy of the *Territorial terrain instructions* for each team and 1 for yourself

Setting

An indoor or outdoor area (preferably with at least 5 m x 5 m of space) that is relatively level and clear of furniture.

Briefing

- Divide the group into teams of approximately equal numbers. Explain that this game simulates negotiating for territorial land space.
- A comet has narrowly missed slamming into planet Earth, but has tilted Earth's axis. Global warming has drastically altered the inhabitable land surfaces on Earth.
- Each team requires land space.
- Clarify the boundaries of the inhabitable space (i.e. the limits you're setting for the playing field). If certain zones within the game parameter need to be out of bounds to participants because of safety or security reasons, you can claim these as United Nations neutral zones and exclude them from the negotiable area. For example, participants cannot trample over an outdoor garden or they must avoid desks or storage cupboards. Check that all teams understand the physical boundaries.
- Distribute the paper, pens, streamers, tape and scissors.

Process

- Tell all teams that they have 10 minutes to:
  1. decide how much space within the designated territory they want to claim for their team without consultation with other teams;
  2. develop a strategy for how they are going to stake out their space using their resources;
  3. secretly map out the space they intend to claim on a sheet of paper. At the end of the 10 minutes, they will be committed to staking their initial claim as per their written map.
- Ask for a volunteer from each team to paraphrase (clarify) their team's understanding of the 3 tasks.
- Hand out the *Territorial terrain instructions* and allow 5 minutes for reading.
- Facilitate rounds 1–4.

Debriefing

- Which is the 'winning' team? Explain that people usually interpret the winner as the team with the most physical space at the end of Round 4. Suggest that when we play a game and 'I win, but you lose', it's likely that you'll play to win next time or you won't want to play any more.
- Should negotiation be all 'take' or should it be 'give and take'?

- Do you gain friends and build business relationships by beating the opponent—making them feel like losers? Is negotiation really a game? Perhaps not, because games produce winners and losers.
- What hindered the success? Assumptions. What were the obvious assumptions? What were the hidden assumptions?
- What's the difference between an assumption and a certainty? They're really educated guesses that need revision from time to time.
- What helped the negotiations?
- What were some of the negotiation strategies used? What were the strengths of some of these? What were the weaknesses of some of these?
- Negotiation is not about how to end up with the biggest slice of pie. It's about creating enough pie for everyone!
- If the outcome of the negotiation doesn't feel good for a stakeholder, the resulting decision isn't likely to last. People's feelings affect their behaviour more than they consciously know or admit.

Territorial terrain instructions

There are 4 rounds:
- Round 1 (5 minutes): Stake out the space as per your map by using the ribbon, tape and scissors.
- Round 2 (10 minutes): Team members clarify the strategies for their negotiation.
- Each team nominates a group representative who will return to the territory and make desired changes, if any, to the claimed terrain. Representatives may discuss their plans and negotiate with other representatives during this round.
- Round 3 (5 minutes): Teams reconvene to discuss the results. Representatives may receive coaching, advice, suggestions and/or instructions from other team members at this time.
- Round 4 (10 minutes): All team members will accompany their representatives to the territory and observe as their representative negotiates for them with the other groups' representatives. Only the nominated representatives may negotiate or make adjustments to the team boundaries during this time (i.e. the discussions are between nominated team representatives only; other team members may observe only). 'Time' will be called at the end of this round. All team representatives must agree on final space allocations by the end of the fourth round or *all space will be forfeited*!

18 'What would you know?'

DIANNE KING

TIME 30 min.

Two people take approximately 30 minutes to complete the activity. This does not include the debriefing.

GROUP SIZE 2–8

2–8 people, with equal numbers of teenagers and parents, can be involved in the activity. The facilitator adopts the role of host and directs the action and reads the questions. Alternatively, if there are no facilitator and group members, elect a host.

Description

This activity highlights communication gaps between people who supposedly know each other. By creating a low-threat atmosphere, in which each player faces similar demands on their knowledge of the other player, this activity helps to develop a setting in which both are encouraged to listen carefully to each other and gain an understanding of each other as individual human beings.

Learning opportunity

Communication is an important aspect of our daily lives; however, it is common to hear complaints about people not listening or not caring about what we say. This activity allows participants to test out their listening, questioning, negotiating and talking skills with those closest to them.

Audience

This activity is specifically designed for teenagers and their parents or main carers; however, by adjusting the questions, the activity could be used by couples, friends or relatives.

Resources

You'll need:

- Playing board (use a photocopier to enlarge the copy provided by 150%)
- 8 poker chips or similar small tokens for participants to move around the board (2 each of red, yellow, green, blue)
- At least 25 prepared questions for parents and teenagers which need to be adjusted for other groups (examples of questions for parents and teenagers are provided)

- Pens and answer sheets for each player
- A host to control the activity
- 1 die

Setting

Generally the setting would be in the home environment or perhaps a small group situation in a classroom.

Briefing

Note: This will change according to the characteristics of the particular group involved.

- Where possible, it is preferable that the host is selected by all parties. The host announces that:

> This is an activity for teenagers and parents which is designed to test out and open up communication among everyone. It explores what teenagers may know about their parents or what parents really know about their teenagers. The players take turns to answer questions about each other, and the person who gets to the finish square first stops the activity.
>
> I am your host and I will control the activity and will make the final decision on correct answers. I am an impartial judge.

Process

- Four colours are used on the board—red, blue, green and yellow. These colours each appear in 2 starting positions.
- Each pair of parent and teenager will use the same start colour. This means that both are aiming for the same finish square. For example, if a parent starts on a red triangle, the teenager with whom they are partnered must start on the other red triangle. They are both partners and opponents aiming for the same finish square.
- A die will be thrown to determine who goes first. The person with the highest throw will be first.
- The host reads one question at a time. If the player does not know the answer, they must still attempt some form of written response. The same question is then given to the opposing person (this is the person on the

same start colour). This person must verbally respond to the question and, if this matches the written answer, the writer is deemed correct and moves 1 place forward on the board. Once both partners have attempted to answer a question the host then moves on to the next player and reads a new question from the other lists, and repeats the same procedure.

- The activity continues with alternating questions between the parents and teenagers until one person has reached the finish square.
- Remember that when a written answer does not match a verbal response at all, the writer does not move forward.
- In the event of a disagreement or an answer that is partly correct, the host will adjudicate.
- If all the questions have been read and nobody has reached the finish square, the game will stop and there will be a debriefing to discuss what happened and what everyone has learnt.

Note

After some initial feedback 2 words were changed in this activity. The words 'game' and 'winner' are not used as the activity is intended to help examine communication problems, rather than build up apprehension about playing a 'game' or being upset at the idea of 'losing' when someone else 'wins'. It is about exploring communication processes among people who may be experiencing problems, and about encouraging a search for solutions through the post-activity debriefing.

Debriefing

1. What issues did this activity highlight for you?
2. What did this activity demonstrate about your communication?
3. How did you feel when you did not know the answer or answered incorrectly?
4. How much time do you usually spend talking and listening to each other?
5. How can you strengthen your communication skills?
6. What would anyone like to add to the discussion?

Parents write answers to these questions

1. What is your teen's favourite school subject?

2. How many subjects does your teen do? Name them.

3. How often does your teen have exams?

4. Name 2 of your teen's current best friends from school.

5. Name 2 activities your teen enjoys on a weekend.

6. What are your teen's 2 favourite sports?

7. How much homework does your teen do every week?

8. What are your teen's 2 favourite television shows?

9. What is your teen's favourite main meal?

10. What is your teen's favourite drink?

11. How does your teen travel to school and how long does it take?

12. What career does your teen want?

13. What results does your teen expect to get from school?

14. How many students in your teen's form?

15. What is the name of your teen's favourite teacher?

16. When your teen is angry he/she usually says. . .

17. What is your teen's favourite saying?

18. What does your teen do once he/she gets home from school?

19. What does your teen think about smoking?

20. What is your teen's favourite CD?

21. What does your teen think about finding a job?

22. What is your teen's favourite pastime?

23. How often does your teen clean his or her bedroom?

24. Which of your habits annoys your teen most?

25. Which 2 things that you do please your teen?

Teenagers write answers to these questions

1. What is the name of the business where your parent works?

2. Where does your parent work (street name and suburb)?

3. What is the full name of your parent's manager/supervisor?

4. What day does your parent do the supermarket shopping?

5. Name 2 sports that your parent enjoys playing.

6. Which of your habits annoys your parent most?

7. Which 2 things that you do please your parent?

8. What are 3 household rules?

9. Where was your parent born and in what year?

10. What are 2 things your parent enjoys about his or her job, today?

11. What are 2 things your parent hates about his or her job, today?

12. What year did your parent begin his or her current job?

13. How many jobs has your parent had?

14. What type of car does your parent drive?

15. In what year did your parent marry?

16. Why does your parent have rules for when you go out with friends?

17. Who makes the main decisions in your house?

18. Why does your parent ask you to do household jobs?

19. What are 2 jobs you must do when you get home from school?

20. Who mainly does the evening dishes?

21. Who does most of the food preparation?

22. What is your parent's favourite food?

23. What is your parent's favourite drink?

24. What are your parent's 2 favourite television shows?

25. How do/can you earn money from your parent?

26. When your parent gets angry with you, he/she usually says. . .

27. What is your parent's favourite saying?

Game board

TEEN ANSWER Question: My answer:	TEEN ANSWER Question: My answer:
TEEN ANSWER Question: My answer:	TEEN ANSWER Question: My answer:
TEEN ANSWER Question: My answer:	TEEN ANSWER Question: My answer:
TEEN ANSWER Question: My answer:	TEEN ANSWER Question: My answer:
TEEN ANSWER Question: My answer:	TEEN ANSWER Question: My answer:

PARENT ANSWER Question: My answer:	PARENT ANSWER Question: My answer:
PARENT ANSWER Question: My answer:	PARENT ANSWER Question: My answer:
PARENT ANSWER Question: My answer:	PARENT ANSWER Question: My answer:
PARENT ANSWER Question: My answer:	PARENT ANSWER Question: My answer:
PARENT ANSWER Question: My answer:	PARENT ANSWER Question: My answer:

19 How to be an egg-spert!

SALLY JEFFRY

TIME 30 min.

Allow at least 30 minutes:
- Time limit of 10 minutes for completion of the activity
- Allow up to 20 minutes for debriefing

GROUP SIZE 2–4

Minimum of 2 people and a maximum of 4 people per team. If used with a larger group, each sub-group must consist of no more than 4 people.

Description

An activity involving a degree of dexterity, but mainly requiring creative team-based problem-solving skills. An apparently complex array of items is presented to the team with similarly 'complex' instructions. Time and patience, and an ability to work together and listen carefully to each other are the key ingredients for success.

Learning opportunity

A teamwork activity which encourages players to 'think outside the square' while working together. An especially good activity when you want to involve players in a physical task that combines both some dexterity and intensive co-operation.

Audience

This activity is suitable for almost any group where teamwork, creativity and problem solving are important.

Resources

Note: This list of resources describes the materials needed for each team of 2–4 players. Where you have more teams, additional sets of resources will be required for each team.

You'll need:

- Playing mat, as per the example (laminate the mat or put a clear plastic cover on it to make it more durable)
- 2 vessels similar to an egg cup but preferably taller and giving the appearance of instability (e.g. 2 tall thin plastic wine glasses with a circumference at the top no larger than a normal sized egg). These vessels are referred to

as the 'yellow' and 'purple' vessels but can be any 2 different colours, according to what is available
- 1 raw egg (with a blue dot on one end and a red dot on the other)
- 1 stick/skewer 25 cm long (e.g. a bamboo satay skewer is most suitable)
- 1 elastic band just large enough to fit snugly around the egg
- 1 piece of string/twine 15 cm long
- Newspaper or plastic to protect the table top from breakages!
- Clock, watch or timer
- Sticky tape

Setting

When only 1 group is involved you need a single table large enough so that everyone can sit around it without touching each other and can also move around the table. Larger groups will require sufficient space to meet this criteria for each sub-group.

Briefing

Announce that this activity will challenge participants' problem-solving skills and is achievable. It has been done by previous teams in less than 10 minutes, so this is the time limit they face. Read out the aim and rules (as set out below) and invite them to 'meet the challenge of becoming "egg-sperts"'!

Process

Before introducing the activity, ensure that everything is set up as follows:

- Place the newspaper or plastic on a flat table and spread it out so it will protect the table from spillage if the egg breaks. You may need to stick down the edges of the paper to prevent it from moving around as the game is being played.
- Place the game board on top and in the centre of the newspaper or plastic. You may also need to stick down the edges of the game board to the newspaper to stop it from moving/sliding as the game is being played.
- Put the 'purple' vessel on the 'purple' square and the 'yellow' vessel on the 'yellow' square.
- Put a blue dot at one end of the egg and a red dot at the other.
- Place the elastic band around the cup of the 'yellow' vessel just below the lip.

- Place the egg in the 'yellow' vessel with the blue dot face down into the vessel.
- Place the skewer and string on the game board in between the 2 vessels.

Aim

Announce that the aim of the activity is to transfer the egg from the 'yellow' vessel to the 'purple' vessel with the egg being inverted (to show blue end) before being placed on the 'purple' vessel using only the tools supplied.

Rules

- The vessels, egg and elastic band must not be touched by any part of the body of any team member at any time during the game.
- The egg must not be damaged or cracked during the game. The game is over if the egg is damaged in any way.
- The elastic band must be used.
- No other materials are to be introduced or used for the game other than the materials provided—for example, using a glove to prevent a 'hand' touching the egg is not allowed.
- The vessels must not be moved out of the squares on which they are placed.
- The newspaper under the game must not be used as part of the game. It is there only to protect the table.

Debriefing

- What happened?
- How did you arrive at your solution?
- What were you feeling at different times through the last 10 minutes?
- How can you relate the problem-solving strategies that you used here to problems in your workplace?

Notes for the facilitator

Some solutions

- Break the stick/skewer in half and gently move the elastic band up on to the egg. Use the 2 skewers carefully as 'chopsticks' on the elastic band, which is now around the egg. The elastic band provides a suitable surface with friction to allow players to 'grip' the egg with the pieces of the skewer. Gently lift, invert the egg and place it in the purple vessel.
- Another option is similar to the above solution: place the egg gently on the game board and manoeuvre the egg until the blue dot is facing up. Pick up the egg with the 'chopsticks' and place it in the purple vessel.

- A third solution involves breaking the stick/skewer into 4 pieces. Two or more of the team members can manoeuvre the sticks until they are underneath the elastic band on the glass (i.e. the 4 sticks will have to be equidistant around the elastic band to create '4 sides'). The team members can then apply pressure to the sticks by gently pulling outwards which will lift the elastic band from the vessel. The elastic band is then moved carefully towards the egg and released onto the egg just above the lip of the vessel (i.e. in the middle of the egg). Leave the sticks inside the elastic band and use them to lift the egg, and either rest it on the board to invert it or invert it in the air before placing it in the purple vessel.
- If the elastic band is a little loose around the egg, the sticks can be twisted without touching the egg to tighten the elastic band on the egg.

General notes

- This game was designed as a fun and relatively quick game to introduce the topic of problem solving in teams. Depending upon different learning styles, there are a number of processes that the team members may use to solve the game. They may sit and discuss various options before starting, pick up the material and have a go, one team member may take over as leader, or they all might talk at once and all might want to have a go.
- As facilitator, it is important to observe the processes of the team as they solve the problem—that is, their communication process, leadership and team membership strategies, learning styles, etc.
- What happens if a team member is able to solve the problem almost immediately? If this happens, it is important to acknowledge the success of the 'team'. You may then like to steer the debriefing straight into the process of solving the problem—for example, how did the other team members feel when the member solved the game so quickly and all by themselves? Would they have liked to contribute to the solution? How did the team member

who solved the problem feel? Have there been situations at work that may be similar to this experience?

- As this activity is relatively flexible, it can accommodate a number of options to provide a different focus for the game. Some of these options are listed below.

Disabilities

The facilitator may choose to give some or all the team members a certain disability prior to the game. For example, one person cannot see but can talk, another person cannot talk but can see while yet another person can see and talk; or all team members can only use their right hands, etc. This will test the dexterity and skill of the team members and will add another dimension to the problem-solving process. This can substantially increase the time required to complete the activity.

Leadership

The facilitator can choose to give a leadership role to a team member or a team member may volunteer for the role, prior to the game. The facilitator may also choose to make the role a directive or consultative role. After the game has finished the team can discuss and reflect on the processes of the leadership and team membership roles during the game.

Competition

A sense of competition can be instilled by setting up 2 or 3 games to run simultaneously in the room. Competition can increase the pressure of teams to perform and can have an effect on the problem-solving and team processes of the members involved. These pressures can be reflected upon and discussed after the game has finished and can be related to workplace situations.

How to be an egg-spert!

Playing mat

YELLOW YELLOW YELLOW YELLOW YELLOW YELLOW YELLOW YELLOW YELLOW YELLOW YELLOW

PURPLE PURPLE PURPLE PURPLE PURPLE PURPLE PURPLE PURPLE PURPLE PURPLE PURPLE PURPLE

**A quick and fun
problem-solving activity**

20 Whose rules are these anyway?

YOLANDA DE WINTER

TIME 30 min.

A minimum of 30 minutes. The discussion may take longer if the facilitator moves it into more specific consideration of actual organisational practices and ways to reassess the relevance of particular behaviours and 'rules'.

GROUP SIZE 12

At least 12 participants, preferably at similar levels in the organisation.

Description

An activity which uses an ambiguous set of rules to generate understanding about how people develop and automatically use rules for behaviour which are neither questioned nor often even evident as influencing behaviour.

Learning opportunity

This activity helps to generate discussion about hidden assumptions in organisations. It is designed to encourage participants to make explicit some of the rules and values which may be taken for granted within their workplace. It can be especially useful when discussion of organisational culture is appropriate (e.g. in a situation of change).

Audience

Any group of adults who are facing changes to routines and familiar behaviours. They may be entering a 'restructuring' phase in their organisation's development, or about to be 'merged' with another work group or organisation.

Resources

You'll need:

- 10 clear plastic drink cups
- 10 wooden drink stirrer sticks
- 2 bowls
- Enough sweets (Smarties, M&Ms or similar sweets) to fill each bowl
- 2 *Observer instruction* sheets
- 1 wristwatch

Setting

This is best done in a large room, with at least 4 tables and chairs, which can be moved around the room. During the activity 2 tables are placed in the centre of the room and at least 2 other tables placed at opposite corners of the room. This is best done before starting the activity. The chairs are placed out of the way during the action, and then moved into a circle or comfortable seating arrangement for the debriefing.

Briefing

- Introduce the activity using the name 'Cupsticks' (it is important not to give unnecessary cues about the issues which may be discussed later).
- Be vague and non-specific about its purpose. You may suggest it is an activity to raise the energy level in the room prior to the next session; or that it seems to have different purposes and may, 'on this occasion', help the group develop a better understanding of the issues being addressed in the workshop in which it is being used.
- Emphasise that it is a short activity requiring some hand–eye co-ordination.

Process

- Ask for 2 volunteers to be observers. Give them their *Observer instruction* sheets and a pen, and ask them to remain beside you while you organise the activity.
- Ask the remainder of the group to divide themselves into 2 equal sized teams.
- Give each participant a cup and a stick.
- State that their task is to *use the stick to pick up the sweets from the bowl and put them in the cup.*
- Read these rules of the game aloud (do not give out any copies).
  - The different coloured sweets have different values.
  - You must use the stirrer stick to pick up the sweets.
  - You can only touch the sweets with the stick.
  - Don't eat any of the sweets during the game.
  - The cup and the bowl must remain on the table.
  - Each team member must take a turn.
  - Each turn continues while the team counts to ten.
  - I will tell you when to start the game and when to finish.
  - Both teams have 3 minutes to practise.

- *Note*: Avoid answering any questions, and re-read the rules only if requested.
- Assign an observer to each team.
- Allocate each team to their 'practice' table at opposite sides of the room. (You may wish to use separate rooms for the practices session—if they are available.)
- After the practice, ensure that all cups are emptied back into the bowls, and then place the bowls on each of the 2 tables in the centre of the room. Look at your watch and then say 'begin *now!*' While you have not actually specified the duration of the activity, this behaviour creates the impression of a 'time limit' and will be read as such by most participants who will therefore try to be as fast as possible.
- Allow about 5 minutes for the action, but you can call 'time' earlier if necessary (e.g. as soon as one bowl is empty).

Debriefing

- Focus your first questions on what happened during each stage of the activity, including the practice.
- Take note of any comments such as: 'We thought we couldn't do that, so we...' and remember to return to these remarks later on.
- Once participants have described their actions, move on to asking how they felt about the activity, again noting reaction to both explicit and unwritten rules.
- Ask the observers to provide their feedback on what they observed. This will be related to the rules that the participants assumed or constructed in the activity.
- At this point you must acknowledge that the activity is actually about unwritten rules and values. Using the comments you noted above that were being used by the participants, and the observers' remarks, ask questions to clarify what was happening, and why the rules are *assumed*.
- Ask whether these rules were invented by the participants, or are they rules that generally exist in the organisation (or society) and that we usually take for granted and do not notice. What values underpin them?
- Finally lead the discussion into a more general discussion about the extent to which all organisations have 'unwritten rules' which help to shape the behaviour of those who work there. Usually these are almost unknown— until we focus very carefully on finding out what we 'take for granted' and learn to question them more closely to establish whether they are really helpful (e.g. habits that save time) or can harm us (routines which slow down or impede our performance at work).

Notes for facilitators

Participants usually treat the activity as a competition between teams, with the teams attempting to maximise results for each team member. Teams either work according to more rules than are stated (evidence for the 'hidden rules' which will be noted by the observers) or find creative ways to work around the rules. The debriefing can effectively lead into an analysis of the rules, values and beliefs of the organisation.

Observer instructions

- Your role in this activity is to observe one of the teams during their practice session and their playing of the game itself.
- Please write down your observations of how your team talks about achieving the goal, and how they set about completing the task. You will be asked for your comments after the game.
- Do not take any active role in the game: you are to observe without influencing team behaviour.
- *Do not tell this to anyone else*: The purpose of this game is to reveal some of the unwritten rules and values by which human beings operate. The team you are observing may come up with creative solutions for picking up the sweets—be sure to note these down—but your main role is to record the rules and values that appear to be *assumed* during the activity. These may be signalled by such comments as: 'We must…', 'We ought to…', 'We should…', 'This is the right way…'.
- What were the rules we heard? What if we break the rules?

21 Where is it?

RICHARD SEBEL

Description

A physical activity that enables participants to learn to navigate a large area which they will need to know well in order to describe it to others and give directions for locating specific destinations.

Learning opportunity

- To familiarise groups with the general layout/floor plan of a large site.

Audience

This game was originally designed for information booth staff working in a multi-building, multi-exhibit event. Participants can be adults or children, but mobility, safety and reliance on eyesight must be considered.

Resources

For each participant you'll need:

- Lists of team members
- Maps, floor plans or general layout of the site
- Customised lists of (or clues for) things to find or questions to answer, which should include both mystery and fun
- Small prizes

Setting

The site can be a factory, hotel, restaurant, ship, hospital, other structure or event/exhibition facility.

TIME 60–90 min.
Approximately 60–90 minutes.

GROUP SIZE 20
Approximately 20 people. Groups need to move around while keeping contact with each other, so a maximum of 7 per group is probably appropriate.

Briefing

- State the game objective and issue each participant with a set of resources.
- Explain that the game solutions are found through investigation of the site, which may require some detective work.
- Set an appropriate time for teams to find the answers to as many questions as they can and return to home base.

Process

The game begins when teams set off on their voyage of discovery. The facilitator should remain at home base to support teams if required. Give participants a prize for returning on time.

Debriefing

Teams can discuss their methods and outcomes with other teams with a view to checking their responses and learning from each other. This will depend on how well participants familiarised themselves with the site. An extension to this debriefing would be to illustrate the answers and to show a site map on an overhead slide.

22 Get it? Do it!

CARMEN RICHARDSON AND WAYNE TOWNSON

Description

A learning activity using teamwork, some physical interaction and individual knowledge to shape revision of a set of information.

Learning opportunity

- To revise and reinforce any 4 step process and up to 50 aspects of a training session in a team environment.
- Facilitators will also be able to test learners' knowledge.

Audience

Trainees who will benefit by the:

- practice of piecing together processes (Phase 1);
- checking of answers to questions about the training (Phase 2).

Resources

You'll need:

- Copy of the game board (use a photocopier to enlarge the one provided by 150%)
- 4 playing pieces
- Set of at least 50 questions that will test aspects of the trainees' knowledge of what has been taught

The game board can be created in at least 3 ways:

1. You can copy the game board on to an overhead slide (in which case, you'll also need a projector). Four small paper shapes can act as playing

---

TIME ~20 min.

- Phase 1 (putting the board together): maximum 2 minutes
- Phase 2 (moving around the board): minimum 15 minutes, maximum determined by the instructor who may give notice at any time that the next round will determine the winner

GROUP SIZE 4–16

A minimum of 4 and a maximum of 16. It's preferable that 4 teams play this game; however, if you have only 4 people, 2 teams of 2 will suffice. More than 4 per team may inhibit active involvement by *all* team members.

pieces. Their silhouettes will be displayed on the screen. If you can do this, cut another overhead slide into four irregular pieces and use different colours to mark each piece.

2. You can make your game board by copying the image on to a large piece of cardboard, which you attach to a whiteboard, flip chart or wall. Playing pieces can be made from differently coloured self-adhesive notes.

3. You can create a larger floor plan sized playing board and lay it on the floor. In this case, you could use participants to act as the playing pieces. The game board was originally created to revise information relevant to the finance industry. Customise it as you wish.

To run Phase 1 of the game (putting the board together), you'll need to have cut the game board into 4 pieces and numbered each piece 1–4. Devise a 4 step process for revision. For example, if the process is connecting to the Internet, determine the 4 steps required to connect to the Internet that you want the players to revise.

Setting

The game may be played in any training room. The equipment and space you have in the training room will guide your choice of game board and pieces. For example, in a computer training room stocked with PCs or terminals, you may choose the overhead slide as a game board. If you have a large whiteboard or flip chart, you may choose to attach a cardboard game board to it. If you have access to a large, open space, you may choose the floor plan sized game board.

Briefing

There are 2 parts to the game:

• Phase 1: putting the board together
• Phase 2: moving around the board

Both phases are designed to help in revising what you've been studying.

Process

Where time permits, you can play both phases, but each phase can be played independently.

Phase 1

• Divide the group into 4 teams.
• The group is to piece the game board together by positioning the 4 pieces according to the logical sequence of steps that match your chosen process. Give the participants a list of the 4 steps in a jumbled sequence. Ask them to consider each piece of the game board as 1 of the 4 steps.
• The participants are to decide the correct sequence before piecing the game board together while reciting (and reinforcing) the correct steps in the sequence.

Phase 2

• Issue each team with a playing piece, and establish the order of play.
• Players' moves are not determined by the throw of a pair of dice, but rather by correctly answering questions posed by the facilitator.
• If the team answers a question correctly, they move forward 2 spots.
• If the team answers a question incorrectly, they move back 1 spot. Players cannot move further back than the starting point.

- The winner is the first team to complete the game by moving forward enough places to move off the board (i.e. to land back on start is not quite a win).

Debriefing

- Feedback should be given continuously during the game.
- When questions are answered incorrectly, the correct answer should be given immediately.
- Use the debriefing time to clarify, consolidate, further revise or reinforce any necessary points.

Game board

Get It? Do It!

Go forward 3 spaces	Go back 2 spaces
Go back 3 spaces	Go forward 3 spaces

Go back 3 spaces

Go back 3 spaces

Go forward 3 spaces

Go back to start

Go forward 5 spaces

START

END

© 1999 ELYSSEBETH LEIGH & JEFF KINDER

23 Recapping review

MAREE JALOUSSIS

TIME 45 min.
Timing will depend on the size of the group. As a rough guide, take your estimated group size multiplied by 3 (i.e. 15 people x 3 minutes = 45 minutes).

GROUP SIZE 4–20
Ideally, 2 teams of 2–10 people, but you can have as many as 20 people.

Description

A knowledge review activity that draws on participants' own knowledge to build a set of key questions to revise the content.

Learning opportunity

- To review the content of a workshop using teams, learners' input and interaction.
- Facilitators note and later review information that is assessed as needing additional revision after the first review.

Audience

Any group that needs to recap learning (i.e. it is paramount that the correct information or procedures are learnt).

Resources

You'll need:

- Approximately 40 squares of paper about 10 cm x 10 cm
- 4 boxes clearly labelled *Questions*, *Team A*, *Team B* and *Review*
- As many small sweets as you anticipate questions (possibly about 40)

Setting

A place where people feel comfortable and can see each other.

Briefing

This activity is designed to help revise (recap) the information that has been introduced.

Process

- Allow about 4 minutes for participants to write 2 questions relating to the course content on to separate squares of paper. They can refer to their course notes. (If you have specific areas to revise, you may wish to use coloured paper, whereby the participants write 1 question per colour for each area.)
- All questions are placed in a box marked *Questions* in the middle of the room. Next to the *Questions* box lie 3 other boxes labelled *Team A*, *Team B* and *Review*. You can add your own questions to the *Questions* box to ensure vital areas are checked.
- Divide the room into 2 teams (one on each side of the room) and name one side Team A and the other Team B.
- Any person from Team B begins by picking any question from the *Questions* box and, with a spirit of fun, asking Team A the question. One or more members from Team A may attempt to answer the question.
- The facilitator is games host and adjudicator (i.e. judges whether or not a question is answered correctly).
- If correct, Team A wins its first prize. The prize is placed in the *Team A* box.
- If Team A answers incorrectly, Team B can try to answer and, if correct, the prize is placed in the *Team B* box.
- When neither team answers correctly, the question goes into the *Review* box.
- Alternate the procedure until all questions have been attempted. Questions in the *Review* box are explained by the facilitator before the prizes in each box are counted. The team with the more prizes is declared the winner and prizes are distributed.

Debriefing

Emphasise that consolidation is an important step in moving information from our short-term memories into our medium-term and, later, long-term memory.

Rallycross

MARIA DIMOLIANIS AND SALLY FRIELANDER GORDON

TIME 45–90 min.

From 45–90 minutes, but the game can usually be run in approximately 1 hour.

GROUP SIZE 6–20

From 6 to 20 people.

Description

A board game-based activity to help participants revise their understanding of a knowledge-based session or program.

Learning opportunity

- To consolidate and reinforce learning and to have fun in a non-threatening environment.
- To review any training session and identify gaps in learning from possible previous training sessions.
- To develop action plans that identify practical strategies to help participants use what they have learnt in the workshop at work.
- To set the pace for further training.

Audience

Any learners who will benefit by consolidating key learning points and team-work.

Resources

You'll need:

- 1 copy of the map for each team. Maps can be produced as A4 or A3 size and laminated for repeated use (use the enlarger facility on a photocopier). You can even make larger maps by recreating them on flip chart paper or plastic sheets
- Small model cars make fun game pieces, but you can use many alternatives such as cardboard cut-out cars to represent teams' progress from the starting point through to the freeway homeward. Label the cars A, B, C and/or D, depending on the number of teams you have. For example, for a group

of 6 people you could have 2 x A, 2 x B and 2 x C. A group of 10 people would need 3 x A, 3 x B, 2 x C and 2 x D.
- Written instructions for each team prepared according to the instruction page that follows
- Participant worksheets (copies of the one provided) for each player

Setting

This activity can be used anywhere participants feel comfortable about working in teams and where they can see each other. The maps can be on desks, on the floor or attached to the wall, whiteboard or flip chart.

Briefing

- Ask participants to choose a vehicle.
- Point out that each car has a letter A, B, C and/or D (which will divide the group into teams of 2, 3 or 4 people according to the letter on their car).
- Issue each team with written instructions (see below).
- At various journey points, participants will approach the facilitator for checking and/or advice.
- Read the objective and the first point only (i.e. all cars begin their journey simultaneously).
- This is a rally, not a race! The objective is to help all cars in your team to complete the rally. Carefully work through each step in the process. Be careful to complete each step before continuing.

Process

- Instruct all cars to begin their journey from the starting point simultaneously and proceed towards the roundabout, and remind them to stop at the first landmark on the way.
- Each sub-group sends a delegate to ask the facilitator for the Landmark 1 clue. They then use the clue to identify the landmark.
- All teams continue to work their way ('rally') through the sheet provided, ticking off each stage as they complete it.

Debriefing

Ask participants to:

- consider the purpose of the activity;
- describe the communication processes or techniques used by their team;

- paraphrase the key learning points;
- note the benefits of creating action plans; and
- identify anything they would still like to know more about.

Can participants identify challenges, difficulties and barriers they and their team encountered?

Instructions

- Identify 4 key learning points to which you want participants to pay particular attention.
- Inspect the map and identify, for yourself, the 3 *landmarks* and the *roundabout*. As participants arrive at each point, they are to ask you for a 'clue'. To prepare these, select 4 items and identify the logical one with which to begin the 'rally'. This is the first *key learning point*. Prepare a clue to help teams identify the learning point. For example, if one of your key learning points in a time management workshop is 'Procrastination is a thief of time', prepare a clue—such as 'This delaying tactic steals our time. What is it?'—to help learners identify this point.
- Devise a sequence of clues to be identified at each of the second and third landmarks.
- The fourth learning point occurs at the roundabout to identify a key decision which is central to the content of the workshop. Because it involves making a choice from among competing alternatives, preface this clue with 'Which avenue would you take to…?' For example, if your learning point for a time management workshop is that 'Large projects are best sub-divided into smaller sets of achievable tasks to fit them into our already busy schedules', you could develop a handout similar to the example given in *Roundabout clue* below.

Roundabout clue

Use this as a model to prepare your Roundabout clue.

   Which avenue would you take to fit a large project into an already busy schedule?
(a) Stop all other work and concentrate solely on the large project.
(b) Continue with regular routine jobs and wait for a time when you can fit in the project.
(c) Break the project into smaller, achievable tasks and slot the task with the highest priority into your busy schedule.
(d) Tell all your colleagues and boss that you're too busy.

- In this case, (c) would probably be the best answer.
- Give each team the appropriate response slip according to the choice they announced to you. For example:
(a) Your car has suffered a tyre blow-out. Seek road service assistance. (Try again.)
(b) Go back, you're going the wrong way. (Try again.)
(c) This is the correct answer. You may proceed to the traffic lights.
(d) You're going around in circles. (Try again.)

- When asked about the toll for learning, talk briefly about the fact that skills and knowledge worth learning are worth the toll (i.e. the time and effort it takes to acquire them). Once each team has completed the rally (i.e. has correctly answered all 4 questions), let them know that they've 'paid the toll' and demonstrated the quality of their learning.

Worksheet (1)

Our answer to Landmark 1 is:

_____

_____

_____

_____

☐ Before continuing, check with your facilitator that your answer is correct. If it is incorrect, try again.

☐ At the roundabout, ask your facilitator for the *roundabout* clue sheet.

☐ Choose an avenue from the 4 choices provided—(a), (b), (c) or (d)—on the clue sheet and check with your facilitator before continuing.

☐ When you arrive at the traffic lights, turn left to visit the Black Mountain Observation Tower. While visiting the Tower, list the major learning points that you have gained from the workshop. Don't delay, it's nearly sunset and you must provide the facilitator with legibly written observations before sunset.

Our key learning points include:

_____

_____

_____

_____

☐ After recording your key learning points, there are still 2 more landmarks to visit. Move on to the second landmark and ask for the clues. Identify the landmark.

Our answer to Landmark 2 is:

_____

_____

_____

_____

Worksheet (2)

☐ Check that your answer is correct, then continue your journey. If you are not correct, *stop*, *revive*, *survive* in the picnic area, work out the correct answer and give it to the facilitator to check before moving on.

☐ There's a beautiful sunset ahead. Use the next 10 minutes to identify strategies with which to apply the 'learning points' (from Black Mountain Observation Tower) to your work, then provide the facilitator with a list of legibly written strategies before continuing.

Our strategies for using our learning points in our work include:

_____

_____

_____

_____

☐ You're low on petrol! Make your way to the Motivation Petrol Station. Once there, write down the fuel/motivations (e.g. recognition, reward, money, control, self-development and/or social interaction) you need to do your work effectively. Be prepared to feedback your team's key discussion points after the rally.

Our motivations include:

_____

_____

_____

_____

☐ Wind your way through 5 km of steep road, through rainforest, past a waterfall and onward to the lookout. Enjoy the view!

☐ Now take the time to consider where you've travelled through the training. Use your observations and strategies to develop a *Personal action plan* to use on the job. Consider issues such as:

- what needs to be implemented;
- steps to take;
- resources needed (people, equipment and/or documents);
- costs;
- obstacles to overcome; and
- when you plan to complete the action plan.

☐ When you have completed your action plans, ask the facilitator for any additional advice.

Personal action plan

☐ It's downhill all the way to the next landmark. Send a delegate to ask the facilitator for the Landmark 3 clue and use the clue to identify the landmark.

Our answer to Landmark 3 is:

_____

_____

_____

_____

☐ Check with the facilitator that you've identified Landmark 3 correctly before continuing towards the freeway. If incorrect, try again.

☐ Ask the facilitator for information about the cost of the toll for learning. Use this space to record your notes on the reply:

_____

_____

_____

_____

☐ Your team is now on the freeway, homeward bound! Congratulations. You've completed Rallycross.

Rallycross

start

Landmark 1

Landmark 2

B

roundabout

D

Landmark 3

picnic area

Motivation
Petrol
Station

N

Black Mountain
Observation
Tower

waterfall

rainforest

lookout

A

C

freeway to home

toll

© 1999 ELYSSEBETH LEIGH & JEFF KINDER

25 Learning organisation

TIME 60–90 min.
Approximately 60–90 minutes.

GROUP SIZE 8–28
Four groups with a maximum of 7 per group.

Description

A board game designed to help participants learn more about the theory of learning in organisations.

Learning opportunity

• To promote a learning organisation approach to revising theory, and to practise teamwork, planning and/or organising.

Audience

This game was originally designed for tertiary students in a learning organisation simulation, but is suitable for groups who will benefit from any of the listed outcomes.

Resources

You'll need:

• Copy of the game board enlarged 200% (use a photocopier and its enlarger facility)
• 4 different coins to act as the game pieces
• 4 stacks of game question cards with 1 of 4 functions printed on one side (the other side blank)
• Pens for each team
• 1 pair of die

Setting

An area where team members can discuss questions and sit around the game board.

Briefing

- Divide the group into 4 teams and give each team a role (observing, understanding, responsibility or doing), the appropriate stack of question cards and a coin.
- Explain that they have formed a learning organisation with one objective— to learn to achieve together.
- All teams receive a stack of cards that are blank on one side and have 1 of the 4 functions on the other.
- The 4 functions represent key aspects of people's roles at work:
  - observing: noticing and learning from what is observed;
  - understanding: identifying theories which help explain what is seen/happening;
  - responsibility: accepting personal responsibility for actions and outcomes;
  - doing: taking action to make things happen.
- Each team is to prepare questions for the other teams based on aspects of the team's role in a learning organisation (or as a complete alternative, on specific content that is to be revised/explored).

- Questions must be about their team's role and written on the reverse side of appropriate cards (i.e. a question such as 'Why is it important to accept personal responsibility?' should be written on the reverse side of a *Responsibility* card). Team members may prepare cards individually or as a team.
- Once teams have prepared their question cards, the facilitator arranges 4 stacks of cards, shuffles each stack and places them appropriately on the game board.

Process

The game begins when teams role the dice. The team that rolls the lowest number moves their coin downwards from the starting square, in an anticlockwise direction, according to the numbers shown on the dice. The team with the second lowest number rolls the dice next, the third lowest rolls third and the highest rolls last.

Rules

- When a team lands on an unoccupied square that contains the team's icon, team members take a card from the top of their stack and, as a team, attempt to answer the question regardless of whether another team wrote the question or they wrote the question.
- When a team lands on an unoccupied square that has another team's icon, the team waits until the next round before continuing.
- When a team lands on any occupied square, each team picks a card from the other team's stack and asks the other team a question.
- When a team lands on the **?**, team members can compose a new question and address it to any team or the facilitator.
- When a team lands on the corner square diagonally opposite start, the facilitator has the option to pick a card from any stack and pose the question to the whole group.

Debriefing

The learning organisation (i.e. all teams) lead their own discussion about what happened, what was learnt, and the next step for the learning organisation.

Game cards

Observing

Understanding

Responsibility

Doing

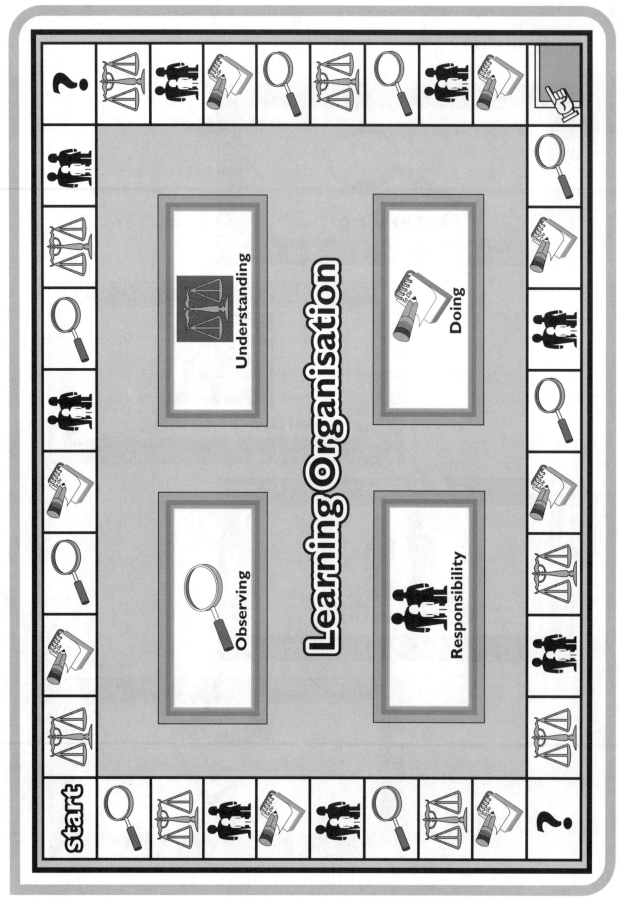

26 What is it?

MAREE ARGY

Description

A review activity involving knowledge of specific computing equipment. The concept can also be applied to equipment of other types.

Learning opportunity

- To identify and locate pieces of equipment that make up a wide area network (WAN). The participants will identify the pieces of equipment from clues about the equipment's purpose or from problems that they may have when administering the network.
- This game is conducted at the end of a training session on troubleshooting on a network. It can be used as a recap and to consolidate key points of a training session and evaluate the success of the training.

Audience

The game is designed for new computer network administrators, with limited or no prior computer experience, who may find terms and concepts overwhelming. Alternatively, the game may be adapted to any technical training course.

Resources

You'll need:

- Instruction sheets and clue sheets (devised by you) with numbered clues for each group. When you're creating these clue sheets, rearrange the lists of clues so that when groups identify a piece of equipment they don't inadvertently give the answer to other groups
- Numbered coloured sheets of paper corresponding to the number of clues on sheets (a different colour for each group)
- Tape (for adhering numbered sheets to the equipment)

TIME 45 min.
An estimated 45 minutes, depending on the number of clues provided to participants.

GROUP SIZE 5+
Unlimited.

Setting

The game area needs to contain the equipment (or pictures of the equipment) to which the clues refer, and allow room for groups to move around freely.

Briefing

- Devise a series of clues for the equipment that participants are to identify. The clues should refer to the purpose of the equipment or problems that may occur with the equipment.
- Form groups of 4 or 5 people. The number of groups is limited only by how many ways you can order the clues so that no 2 groups receive identically ordered lists.
- Give groups the coloured and numbered sheets, tape and clue sheets, along with copies of the instructions (see 'Process' below).

Process

- Read the clues and identify each piece of equipment.
- Write the name of the piece of equipment on the clue sheet.
- Attach the coloured, numbered sheet that corresponds to the clue on the piece of equipment.
- Groups have different clues so the numbers on coloured sheets you see appearing on the equipment will differ (in other words, don't bother attempting to decipher other groups' efforts).
- There may be more than 1 clue that relates to a piece of equipment.

Debriefing

At the end of the game, the facilitator moves to each piece of equipment and asks groups to read the relevant clues and to explain how they reached their conclusions.

27 The essence

RUTH HANBURY

Description

A team-based activity which combines aspects of marketing, creativity and ways in which competition can contribute to team cohesion.

Learning opportunity

- To explore different roles within a team, and ways to generate creativity in teams.
- It emphasises the importance of gathering the facts before proceeding, and demonstrates the adverse results when team members don't work together.

Audience

People who work in teams and may benefit from analysis of team dynamics and creativity.

Resources

The facilitator is to have the following resources available for each team:

- Samples of lavender oil for each team
- 1 *Team instruction sheet* per team
- *Additional information sheets* on lavender oils—methods, uses and target markets
- Burners, candles, matches and massage oils for each team

Setting

An area where the 2 teams can sit and discuss, and work with resources.

> **TIME 40 min.**
> A total of 40 minutes:
> - 10 minutes for briefing before the game commences
> - 20 minutes for the actual game
> - 10 minutes for debriefing at the conclusion of the game

> **GROUP SIZE 14**
> Two teams with no more than 7 per team.

Briefing

Ask participants to think of themselves as new aromatherapy consultants who have just completed their basic product knowledge and sales training. Explain that they are competing for a marketing contract and must use everything they can to produce a creative ad campaign theme for lavender oils.

Process

- Divide the group into 2 teams and call one team Oils·R·Us Pty Ltd and the other team The Essentials Pty Ltd.
- Explain that the 2 companies are competing for the largest market share for sales of aromatherapy oils.
- Show teams a sample of lavender oil.
- Tell teams that oils:
  - must not be taken internally;
  - must not be used if pregnant; and
  - should be used in half the regular concentrate for children.
- Hand a *Team instruction sheet* to each team.
- During the action, provide 1 piece of information or resource at a time and only when requested. Note whether or not teams obtain all resources. Observe how teams function and the roles adopted by members.

Debriefing

Ask teams the following questions:

- How did you come up with your ad?
- Did you consider options?
- Did you use all the available resources?
- What happens if you don't do enough market research or get all the facts?
- What happens if you take too long to decide on a strategy?
- Did you keep an eye on what the competitors were doing?
- Were you creative and, if so, how was it beneficial?
- What were the different roles that evolved in the teams?

Team instruction sheet

Scenario
You are new aromatherapy consultants who have just completed your basic product knowledge and sales training. Your company wants to increase market share for sales of aromatherapy oils more quickly than your opposition company.

Instructions
Your project is to design a 30 second television commercial for essential oil Lavender to increase sales of the product by 50%. You may not communicate directly with your competition.

Additional information and resources
Your facilitator has information on the use of essential oils, your target market and resources such as burners, candles, matches and massage oils that may help you when designing your TV commercial. You may ask the facilitator for only one resource at a time.

Additional information sheet

Lavender oil is good for relieving the symptoms of tension headaches, stress, tension and insomnia. It helps to relax muscles after stress, sport or childbirth. It has a soothing and calming effect on the body, mind and emotions, and can be used in at least 5 ways:

1. in warm water: heated in a burner by a candle to give off vapours;
2. in a warm bath for both vapour and muscle relaxant effects;
3. during a massage, mixed with massage oil;
4. in a foot bath with warm water;
5. directly applied to wounds, burns and abrasions as an antiseptic to reduce pain and to promote rapid healing because it stimulates healthy tissue growth and minimises scarring of damaged tissue.

Market research

There is a huge sales potential in targeting new mothers.

28 Retail ordering and stock control

RICHARD GEORGE EAST

TIME | hour

At least 1 hour: approximately 20 minutes per example with time for briefing and debriefing.

GROUP SIZE 6–12

A minimum of 6 and a maximum of 12 managers. Three groups are prearranged with a minimum of 2 and a maximum of 4 per group. The optimum is 3 per group. Choose team leaders who may require decision-making practice.

Description

A simulation demonstrating how to use normal workplace equipment and business knowledge to help trainees understand the operations of complex retail business operations. The game was designed to be used with specific 'in-house' terminology. You will need to adapt the terminology and examples to suit your needs.

Learning opportunity

- To analyse decision-making processes during re-enacted situations experienced in Heighes Menswear stores.
- To observe participants' practical skills and to explore participants' reasoning behind their decisions on stock levels.

Audience

Retail store managers with more than 2 seasons' experience. This simulation has been designed with a specific, register-based ordering system in mind. The principles of this area of retail trading remain the same, no matter whether the system is automated or is a manual order book system. This simulation can be customised to suit other situations. The critical learning opportunity is to assist managers to examine and compare their approaches to this very profitable area of retail business.

Resources

You'll need your own equipment which equates to:

- Cash registers with full barcode files
- Butcher's paper and marker pens for each group
- 1 copy each of the 3 example handouts for each participant

168

Setting

Care must be taken that registers are placed in separate group areas, thus allowing each group to work without interruption.

Briefing

- Explain the objectives of the simulation and that the butcher's paper and marker pens are to be used to record the reasoning behind the way the orders have been placed.
- Explain each example to the groups, emphasising the type of store, the time of year and possible current weather patterns.
- It is important to mention that *there are no absolute rights and wrongs* in this process; however, it can be useful to receive constructive criticism from others and to achieve a consensus among the entire group as to which way to go.
- Particular attention should be given to the breakdown of garment sizes, colours and styles ordered, and the relationship they have with each other. For example, we know from past experience that for each pair of size 32 black shorts sold, we sell 5 pairs of size 34 blue shorts—in other words the known ratio is 1:5.
- Every participant will have a different experience with stock ordering and the ratios involved. This is bound to create much debate. It is advisable, therefore, to have the executive in charge of stock control present so that arguments that run off on a tangent can be balanced by the facts generated by the company's past experiences.

Process

- Each group discusses the orders they wish to place for the first example. They then record this on the example handout and enter orders in the register.
- Each example should take approximately 20 minutes, after which time everyone is to come together so the results can be compared and each team leader can present the rationale and arguments.

Debriefing

Use the examples, along with case studies, to draw out participants' problems with the system and also any remaining questions about the system that have not arisen in the participants' experiences at store level.

Example 1: Sydney South-West Store

Department 294: Long Leg Ruggers
- Time: first week in December
- Best selling colours: Aqua, Jade, Ocean, Royal, Turquoise
- Medium colours: White, Navy, Silver, Forest
- Poor selling colours: Black, Lemon, Green, Olive, Maroon

Order additional stock for Christmas trading and first week in January when you consider it necessary.

Order through Register Screen.

Colours	Sizes						
	77	82	87	92	97	102	107
White							
Navy							
Black							
Aqua							
Jade							
Lemon							
Ocean							
Royal							
Silver							
Turquoise							
Green							
Olive							
Maroon							
Forest							

Example 2: Sydney Outer West Store

Department 1A: Class 777, Subclass 51—Yakka School Trousers
- Time: 3 weeks before Back To School in January.
- What action would you take to ensure no *out of stocks* in last week prior to school going back and no *out of stocks* 1 week after school goes back?
- Order through Register Screen.

Boy's sizes	Present stock
79	16
81	24
84	24
86	8

Men's sizes	Present stock
77R	15
82R	24
87R	24
92R	12
97R	3
87S	10
92S	14
97S	6
102S	3
107S	3

Example 3: Sydney Inner West Store

Basic Trackpants
- Time: 3 weeks after start of Winter. Current climate warm.

Model	S	M	L	XL	XXL
			Stock		
Navy	6	8	10	6	3
Grey	3	4	5	3	2

- What additional stock (if any) would you order?

Navy
Grey

29

Irish preferences

BARBARA DOBOSZ

TIME 20 min.

Approximately 20 minutes.

GROUP SIZE 6+

Two or more groups with 3–8 people in each group.

Description

A knowledge review activity which helps participants revise their understanding of a particular theoretical framework. With some adjustments to the content, this activity can be used for revising other bodies of knowledge.

Learning opportunity

• To allow participants to review their Myers–Briggs Type Indicator™ preferences. They will discuss aspects of each preference and make a four-leaf clover to take with them that will help them to remember their preferences.

Audience

People who have determined their character preferences using the Myers–Briggs Type Indicator™ process (i.e. they already know their four letters—e.g. ISTJ).

Resources

You'll need:

• 1 set of dice for each group
• 1 green drinking straw
• 1 split-pin for each participant
• 1 set of cards for each participant. Each set consists of 8 green, heart-shaped cards, each with one of the following letters written on one side:
  – E (Extroversion)   – T (Thinking)
  – I (Introversion)   – F (Feeling)
  – S (Sensing)   – J (Judging)
  – N (Intuition)   – P (Perceiving)

Setting

Groups sit at separate tables far enough apart to avoid hearing each other. After the briefing, lively music will energise groups. Participants' notes, from when they determined their preferences, may be nearby for reference.

Briefing

- Place 1 drinking straw, 1 split-pin and 1 set of cards per participant in the centre of each group. These pieces will form the personalised shamrocks.
- Explain that this is an activity to help participants review their understanding of the Myers-Briggs Type Indicator™ theory, and its relevance for them, and to help participants to remember the 4 letters that signify their preferences and what they mean.
- Tell them that you'll explain the process in a moment and allow time for each group to complete all the steps in the process. They may ask you to help them stick to the process, but you will not answer content questions nor adjudicate disputes.

Process

- To choose who rolls the dice first, each group identifies who travelled the farthest from home to the venue. Once this person is identified, he/she throws the dice and has first turn, to be followed by the person sitting on their left (i.e. clockwise), and so on around the circle.
- Participants take turns to throw the dice.
- Each time participants roll 2 even numbers, they can try to win a piece from the centre by making a statement about themselves or their behaviour that reflects 1 of their 4 letters. Thus a participant with a Myers-Briggs Type Indicator™ of ISTJ may choose to try for an 'I' leaf by stating: 'I prefer to work alone or one to one.' This is a statement which accurately reflects an introversion characteristic.
- If participants cannot think of a suitable statement, they forfeit the turn and wait until the next round. On the second attempt, they may consult notes and/or other team members may give single word prompts to assist. If team members believe that a statement doesn't reflect the true spirit of the characteristic, the statement should be discussed. Teams must resolve disputes without reference to the facilitator.
- When either of the dice shows an odd number, a turn is forfeited but, if on the next turn an odd number shows yet again, participants may try for a leaf (i.e. 2 odds make an even on the next round only).

- When participants make accurate statements, they take the leaf from the centre and write the statement they used to win it on the reverse.
- Once participants have 4 leaves (1 from each of the 4 Myers-Briggs Type Indicator™ continuums), they next attempt to gain a straw and then a split-pin.
- Once all team members have earned all 6 pieces (i.e. 4 leaves, 1 straw and the split-pin) they pin the heart-shaped leaves together to make the shape of a four-leaf clover and push the split-pin through one end of the straw which becomes the stem of the four-leaf clover.
- Finally, they spread the split-pin at the back to secure all pieces.

Debriefing

Write comments to the following questions on the board:

- Who would like to comment on what happened in the game?
- Was it fun?
- Was it frustrating?
- How did you feel during the game or afterwards?
- Did everyone clearly identify the Myers-Briggs Type Indicator™ characteristics during the game?
- What did you learn through making statements about characteristics and through listening to others?

30 Approaching safety

GARY SEATON

Description

An activity which helps participants to understand the vital importance of always using—and teaching about—correct safety procedures in workplaces.

Learning opportunity

- To examine the relevance of safety training in organisations and the positive impact on organisational finances that can be attributed to safety training.
- To develop a safety training plan for an organisation.

Audience

Managers, supervisors and team leaders; in fact, anyone responsible for increasing awareness of occupational safety issues.

Resources

You'll need:

- 1 *Briefing sheet* for each participant (including observers)
- Role instructions for 5 players
- 1 *Review sheet* for each observer

To simulate workplace hazards:

- 1 cardboard box placed on a desk to resemble a slitting machine, with a book or something similar to act as a front guard
- 1 soup ladle to pour water into a bucket to resemble molten metal poured into a mould
- 1 box that can be lowered from a height using a string to resemble a 100 tonne press

TIME **1 hour**

Approximately 60 minutes:
- 10 minutes for distribution of information sheets, familiarisation of data and facilitator preparation of simulated equipment
- 5 minutes for actual simulation
- 45 minutes for debriefing

GROUP SIZE 6

A minimum of 6 people (5 who play key simulation roles and at least 1 to act as observer and complete a review sheet). If there are more people, they act as additional observers.

Setting

- The simulation and debriefing can be run within any area free from excessive distractions.
- Have the 3 models set up in an appropriate place before you begin.

Briefing

- Ask for 5 volunteers (one to act as Jerry, another as Kim and 3 as new staff members).
- Distribute a *Briefing sheet* to all participants (including observers).
- Allow up to 10 minutes for the players to familiarise themselves with the scenario.
- Distribute a *Review* sheet to all observers.
- Explain the models and answer any questions.

Process

- Ask Jerry to begin the process.
- Allow 5–10 minutes for the players to act out their instructions. Do not involve yourself in the simulation.

Debriefing

- Ask players how they felt.
- Ask observers what happened.
- Take approximately 45 minutes to consider issues mentioned on the *Review sheet(s)*.
- Involve both observers and players in positive discussion.

Briefing sheet

- You're part of a medium-size manufacturing company employing 100 people.
- There are a number of technical manufacturing processes that require slitting large rolls of copper, fabricating moulds from molten metal and positioning large metal items under an industrial press.
- The team leader, Jerry, has employed 3 new staff members.
- Each new staff member was allocated a task by Kim.
- None of the new staff members was given instructions regarding machinery or safety.
- The team leader was racing to a meeting when the new staff members began work.
- Kim assumed they knew the machinery and safety procedures.

Review sheet

About the role play

1. What comments would you make about the manner in which Jerry inducted the new team members?
2. What suggestions would you make to improve the induction process?
3. What advice would you give to actual new staff members to ensure such incidents do not occur?

About the safety issues

1. How could the injuries have been prevented?
2. What is the impact on the employees' wages in relation to the accidents?
3. What implications are there for management regarding the injuries these employees have suffered? What are the associated costs of these accidents? How will they impact on the bottom line of the organisation?
4. What suggestions do you have for improving safety in your workplace?

Jerry

- You're the team leader for your section.
- You're very focused on your aspirations to become the superintendent of your shift.
- Personnel has asked you to induct 3 new team members to your shift.
- After introducing yourself to the new staff members, you must attend a meeting with the Superintendents' Review Board to determine your suitability for promotion. This is the moment you've been waiting for! You have no choice but to tell Kim to take responsibility for the new staff members while you attend the review board meeting.
- Coincidentally, Kim commenced work in your section only last Monday.
- The simulation begins when you introduce the 3 new staff members to Kim.

Kim

- You'd like to show the new employees what you know, and also have them believe that you're a person of importance in the team. You allocate New Staff Member 1 to the slitting machine, New Staff Member 2 to the metal mould and New Staff Member 3 to the die press.
- You then go to the canteen for morning tea.
- The simulation begins when Jerry introduces you to the new staff.

New Staff Member 1

- You're 18 and have recently graduated from high school.
- This is your first job.
- You're naturally inquisitive and feel inclined to touch every piece of machinery you see, no matter how technical.
- Kim has allocated you the task of operating the slitting machine, which you assure him you're capable of operating.
- You have no idea what you're doing. You flick a switch, attempt to remove the front guard and cut off the top of your finger.
- The simulation begins when Jerry introduces you to Kim.

New Staff Member 2

- You're a 54-year-old migrant with limited English. You can read only basic English and cannot yet write in English.
- You've been unemployed for 3 years. You're eager to please and show how good an employee you can be.
- You jump in to start any task without hesitation.
- Kim has asked you to operate the die machine and pour molten metal into moulds. You've never handled molten metal before and on your first attempt at pouring a mould, you poor molten metal over your elbow.
- The simulation begins when Jerry introduces you to Kim.

New Staff Member 3

- You're a 48-year-old accountant with no experience in a manufacturing environment.
- You're extremely wary around heavy technical equipment.
- Your accountancy business has collapsed and you have substantial debts. You're in grave danger of the bank foreclosing on your loan and simply cannot afford to be unemployed.
- Kim allocates you the task of operating the 100 tonne press.
- You watch another operator working another press and decide it is all too much.
- You turn and accidentally hit your head on the press.
- The simulation begins when Jerry introduces you to Kim.

31

What *bugs* you about a meeting?

PETER BAINBRIDGE

TIME 20–40 min.

Approximately 20–40 minutes.

GROUP SIZE 2+

2 or 3 people or 2 or 3 teams.

Description

A board game which introduces effective meeting procedures and helps participants understand how they can contribute to effective meetings.

Learning opportunity

- To provide newcomers to meeting procedures with a chance to consider some of the potential problems that may occur before, during and after a meeting.
- To establish good practices when planning meetings.

Audience

People who haven't had extensive experience in conducting meetings or those who would like to refresh their meeting techniques and increase their awareness of possible problems.

Resources

You'll need:

- 1 copy of the playing board enlarged 200% on a photocopier
- Cut outs of the playing tokens (below), which you can copy on to different coloured paper or cardboard.

Setting

An area where the board can be set with cards in place, and players can sit and discuss cards without interruption.

Briefing

- Explain that this is an awareness game to allow players the opportunity to experience, discuss and reflect on factors that make a meeting work well.
- Ask for a volunteer or nominate 1 person (or team representative) to take the role of the chairperson (C).
- Nominate another person (or team representative) to take the role of the meeting secretary (S).
- Nominate a final person (or team representative) to take the role of the meeting member (M).
- Display the playing board and explain that each space represents **5 minutes** of elapsed meeting time.

Process

- Players take turns to move to the next space in the following order: chairperson, secretary, then member.
- Players can move 1 square forward, left or right, provided the space is not occupied by another player.
- When a player lands on a bug, a card is taken from the top of the pile. The player comments on how the statement on the card affects meetings. The player then moves the token according to the instructions on the card.
- Cards are returned to the bottom of the pile unless the letter on the card matches a player's token, in which case the player keeps the card for a bonus point calculated at the end of the game.
- When the first player reaches the end, this player keeps 4 bonus cards (regardless of the letter on the card).
- All players count their cards and the player with the most cards wins.

Debriefing

Ask each player:

- Which comments were most meaningful and why?
- How do the events described on the cards affect the success of meetings?

The chairperson maintained control and ensured that discussions didn't become overheated

Move forward, left or right 10 minutes

Dynamic discussion bonus!

Move forward, left or right 10 minutes

Dynamic discussion bonus!

Move forward, left or right 10 minutes

The topics and objectives have been clearly stated

Move forward, left or right 15 minutes

The topics discussed have been well researched

Move forward, left or right 15 minutes

Someone's mobile phone rings

Move back 5 minutes

The emergency evacuation alarm sounds during the meeting

Move back 10 minutes

A social lunch drags on

Move back 10 minutes

The chairperson prepares clear, concise, informative and challenging discussions

Move forward, left or right 10 minutes

The minutes of the last meeting are accurate, requiring no amendments

Move forward, left or right 15 minutes

Summarised reports are presented

Move forward, left or right 15 minutes

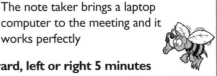
The note taker brings a laptop computer to the meeting and it works perfectly

Move forward, left or right 5 minutes

Budget discussions overrun allocated time frames

Move back 10 minutes

Another group turns up at the door expecting to be able to use the room

Move back 5 minutes

Coffee spills on to important documents

Move back 5 minutes

  The agenda is adhered to

Move forward, left or right 5 minutes

 Appropriate time limits are nominated for discussions points

Move forward, left or right 10 minutes

  The meeting attendees decide to take a *working* coffee/tea break

Move forward, left or right 10 minutes

 All members of the meeting can see and hear each other easily

Move forward, left or right 15 minutes

  Chairperson has a hangover and is feeling a bit *under the weather!*

Move back 5 minutes

 Meeting starts on time

Move forward, left or right 10 minutes

  The secretary has arranged sandwiches and orange juice for a *working lunch*

Move forward, left or right 15 minutes

 Meeting starts 10 minutes late

Move back 10 minutes

 Members takes time to read the report word for word while others chat about the weather

Move back 10 minutes

 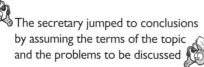 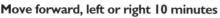 The secretary jumped to conclusions by assuming the terms of the topic and the problems to be discussed

Move forward, left or right 10 minutes

  The discussion moves away from the topic and everyone loses the plot

Move forward, left or right 5 minutes

  The agenda was not sent out prior to the meeting

Move back 5 minutes

   A disagreement has developed in the meeting with the member threatening to walk out

Move back 5 minutes

Minutes of previous meeting not accurate—amendments required

Move back 10 minutes

 Venue too small

Move back 10 minutes

 The venue was changed and all members were notified on time

Move forward, left or right 10 minutes

Poor lighting in the meeting room

Move back 5 minutes

 Decisions are being documented concisely

Move forward, left or right 10 minutes

The venue was changed, but most of the members were not notified on time

Move back 15 minutes

 Morning tea becomes an extended social chat

Move back 10 minutes

The overhead projector globe blows and a replacement is unavailable

Move back 5 minutes

 Dynamic discussion bonus!

Move forward, left or right 10 minutes

The chairperson asked questions that provoked lateral thinking and stimulated information exchanges

Move forward, left or right 10 minutes

 The chairperson ignores obviously flawed and incorrect information to be documented in the minutes

Move forward, left or right 15 minutes

The whiteboard was full of markings from a previous meeting and no eraser was available

Move back 5 minutes

 Sexist comments and improper gender references were made

Move back 5 minutes

Frustrating interpersonal bug: a distracting trait in another person that you must simply ignore

Don't move till next turn!

Game board

What bugs you about a meeting?

Stack cards here

C S M

32
Coloured names

GILLIAN SEILS

TIME 20–40 min.

Approximately 20–40 minutes, depending on the size of the group.

GROUP SIZE 8–36

From 8–36 people.

Description

A quick 'warm-up' activity which can help people to relax and feel comfortable in a new or unfamiliar situation.

Learning opportunity

This game helps participants in a conference, workshop or other program get to know one another.

Audience

This exercise can be used early on the first day of longer programs. It assists participants to build a rapport with one another. It also provides a grouping technique for future team-building exercises.

Resources

You'll need:

- Whiteboard or flip chart paper and markers
- Thick black pens for participants
- Enough coloured self-adhesive notes (approximately 7.5 cm x 7.5 cm) to divide the whole group into sets of 4–6 people. For example, 16 people will require 4 different colours for 4 teams each of 4 people

Setting

Any room with a flat floor and movable furniture.

Briefing

Write 3 relevant questions that are to be answered and discussed by group participants on the whiteboard or flip chart. The questions can range from general topics—for example:

• What is your favourite colour?
• Who are you?
• Why are you here?
• What do you want to learn?

to more course specific topics for a team-building workshop—for example:

• What is one positive characteristic you bring to a team?
• What would you prefer to avoid?
• What do you want the team to achieve?

Process

• Give each participant a brightly coloured self-adhesive note. Ask them to write their name on it with black pen and stick it on themselves.
• Ask participants with the same coloured note to group together and answer the 3 questions. Allow 5 minutes for interaction.
• Ask participants to speak to people with a different colour for a few minutes and discuss their responses to the questions. Continue until all colour groups have had a chance to meet.

Debriefing

• What interesting things were learnt during the various discussions?
• Did anyone feel threatened by the exercise? What made it threatening?
• Do you now feel more like a team? How did this sharing of ideas help? (Or, if the answer is 'no', how do you feel?)
• How does this exercise represent what happens when a team first comes together?

33 Say hullo

RAY MORTLOCK

TIME 10 min.
At least 10 minutes for a group of 15 people.

GROUP SIZE 15
Ideally, this activity requires at least 15 people.

Description

A more active process requiring participants to move about in order to meet everyone in a new or unfamiliar setting.

Learning opportunity

• To create a friendly and informal learning environment.

Audience

Participants who do not already know each other and who may feel threatened by a formal introductory process.

Resources

You'll need:

• Clear plastic clip-on or pin-on name tag holders for all participants
• Name tag cards (2 per participant) and pens or pencils

Setting

Participants must be able to intermingle with relative freedom of movement.

Briefing

• Participants are given a name tag holder and 2 card inserts each. They are requested to write their first name (or the name by which they're known) on one card and their last (or family) name on the other card.
• The cards are collected and redistributed in a manner that ensures that participants now have 2 cards, neither of which is their own.

Process

Participants now mingle, introduce themselves, compare and swap cards until they find their 2 original name cards. They can swap only 1 card at a time in an effort to retrieve their own 2.

Debriefing

- How did this exercise help you get to know other participants?
- What methods did you use to negotiate for the retrieval of your card?
- Which was easier—to circulate and swap cards without discussion or to discuss the process?

34 Famous faces

SUZANNE VUCUROVIC

GROUP SIZE 20

Generally, up to 20, but larger groups can be divided into smaller sub-groups.

Description

A word game which encourages people to talk and also help them learn about their fellow participants.

Learning opportunity

• To help participants to relax and feel comfortable when asking questions.

Audience

This game was originally designed for people for whom English is a second language. It can also be used with most groups who are beginning any learning process and do not know each other.

Resources

You'll need:

• Stickers with the names of famous people printed on them, or photos of famous people
• A small prize for each participant

Setting

Enough room for participants to stand in a circle facing each other.

Briefing

Tell everyone that they will have a person's name (or photo) placed on their back. Their task will be to ask questions that will help them guess whose name (or photo) they are wearing.

Process

- The facilitator moves around the circle, placing a sticker or photo on the back of each participant.
- The first player (the one who has a name/photo placed on their back first) turns around so the name or photo of the famous person is visible to the group.
- The player asks one closed question at a time to help them determine whose name or photo is on their back (e.g. 'Am I a woman?').
- The rest of the group may only answer 'yes' or 'no'.
- After each player has received an answer to their question, they turn around to face the circle again and it is the next player's turn.
- Each player in the circle has a turn and the process continues until everyone has guessed whose name or photo they are wearing.
- When a participant correctly guesses their famous person, they win a small prize.

Debriefing

- What kinds of questions were most helpful in getting information?
- What other kind of questions could help them find out more quickly? ('Open' questions are more useful than 'closed' ones and this exercise can be used to introduce the difference between these kinds of questions.)
- How did different players solve the problem of finding out the name on their back?
- Did anyone feel threatened by the exercise and, if so, why?

35 Getting to know you

SANDRA WOOD

TIME 30–60 min.

30–60 minutes, depending on the size of the group.

GROUP SIZE 15

Up to 15 people.

Description

This activity uses an interview/survey format to collect information about participants for sharing with the group.

Learning opportunity

This activity provides an opportunity for group members to meet each other in an informal way, learn a little about each other and, most importantly, learn each other's names. It is good for courses requiring teamwork, group processes and co-operation.

Audience

A group working together for 2 days or longer. The game is best for groups coming together for the first time or groups where the participants don't know each other well.

Resources

You'll need:

- Pens and paper
- A prepared question card for each group member, including the facilitator, with a different question on each card. Here are some sample questions:
  - What is your favourite movie (or book) and why?
  - If you could have any job you'd like, what would it be?
  - You've just won the lottery. What are you going to do now?
  - If you could go anywhere you like for a holiday, where would you go and why?
  - What type of car would you like to drive?
  - Name 2 achievements of which you are proud.

- If you could trade places with anyone in the world, who would it be and why?
- If asked, what would your best friend say about you?
- What are your interests and/or hobbies?
- If you could do absolutely anything you'd like for one day, what would you do?

Setting

Either in an indoors training environment or outdoors. You'll need tables and chairs in both settings and clipboards if you're conducting the activity outdoors.

Briefing

- Introduce the activity to participants as an opportunity to get to know each other.
- Mention the importance of using the name by which a person likes to be called and the benefits of working together in teams (i.e. people can achieve more in teams than they can individually).
- Encourage a friendly, light-hearted atmosphere.
- Emphasise that they will be asked to correctly recall the names of everyone they talk to.

Process

- Hand out pens, a sheet of paper and a question card to each participant.
- Ask participants to read their question to themselves and to write their own answer on the top of their sheet of paper.
- Everyone then begins to move around, find a partner and introduce themselves, then say: 'Do you mind if I ask …' (e.g. '…what is your favourite movie or book? Why is that?'). They then add that person's name and answer to their sheet of paper. The other person then asks their question and records the name and the answer.
- Participants continue to circulate until everybody has names and responses from all present.
- The facilitator keeps note of progress and, when everyone has completed the task, asks the group to re-form and sit in a circle so everybody can see each other.
- The facilitator then reintroduces him/herself, reads out the questions on the icon sheet and all the answers they collected—for example:

> My name is Sandra and my question was: 'What is your favourite movie or book and why?' My favourite movie was *Out of Africa* because I loved the scenery, the music and the clothes. Steve [looking at Steve] liked *The Mask* because he thought it was very funny. Mary [looking at Mary] liked…etc.

- It is important to model brief answers and ask everyone to be concise.
- After all participants have read out their sheets, do a quick quiz. Ask who thinks they can go around the group and remember everyone's name without looking at their sheet. Applaud the efforts of all volunteers.
- Alternatively, you can delay this quick quiz and use it later as a stand-up energiser.

Debriefing

- What did you notice happening throughout the activity?
- How did you feel at the start of the activity? How do you feel now?

Worksheet

Course title	
Venue	

I am:

My question is:

My answer is:

I asked:	Who said:
1	
2	
3	
4	
5	
6	
7	
8	
9	
10	
11	
12	
13	
14	

36

Whom am I meeting?

CAROL SHAW

TIME 35 min.

Up to 35 minutes:
- 5 minutes (approx.) for the briefing
- 5 minutes for the game
- An average of 1 minute per participant when they introduce their partner to the whole group
- 5 minutes (approx.) for the debriefing

GROUP SIZE 20

Up to approximately 20 people.

Description

An activity which uses an interview process to help participants learn more about one other person and use that knowledge to introduce them.

Learning opportunity

- To help participants know each other better.
- To reduce barriers that may exist because of shyness, etc.
- To take pressure off participants and the facilitator by introducing a task focused activity that incorporates introductions.

Audience

The game is best for groups coming together for the first time or groups where the participants don't know each other well.

Resources

You'll need:

- Pens
- Questions that have been printed on 2 distinctly contrasting coloured papers

Setting

Anywhere with sufficient space for people to move around easily.

Briefing

- Issue sheets of one coloured paper to one half of the group and the other colour to the other half of the group.

- When instructed, participants cross the room and pair up with a person holding a different coloured handout. They introduce themselves and find a space in which they can be reasonably comfortable for 4 or 5 minutes.
- Allow 2 minutes for each person to interview the other. They are to obtain answers to questions in the handout.
- They will later read these answers aloud to the whole group to introduce the person they interviewed.
- Encourage participants to remain focused on their task because they'll have only 2 minutes for their interviews.

Process

- Brief the whole group.
- Allow time for participants to find partners and settle down.
- Announce when the first 2 minutes starts.
- Announce when the second 2 minutes starts.
- Keep the pace brisk. Clearly announce the end of the first 2 minute period. Remind everyone that the first interview is ended and that the interviewer must become the interviewee.
- Announce the end of the second 2 minute period and ask participants to return to their original seat rather than remaining with their partner.
- Ask for volunteers to introduce the person they interviewed. Each person must state the name of the person they interviewed and report their responses to the questions. There is not a lot of stress involved because everyone is talking about someone else, and not about themselves. Ask the person being introduced to stand while this introduction is taking place.
- Repeat this process until everyone has been introduced.

Debriefing

- Did everyone feel more relaxed after the game?
- Did it help to lower communication barriers?
- As a facilitator, reflect on whether or not pressure was taken off the participants and yourself, and whether or not the game offered you insights into participants' attitudes or reactions.
- Did you establish credibility?
- Ask for the return of the handouts. This allows the facilitator to record audience expectations before the workshop commences. These can be linked to a similar handout to record feelings about outcomes at the conclusion of the workshop.

Handout

Name

Favourite hobbies

Sporting or recreational preferences

Favourite colour

What benefits are you expecting to achieve from attendance at this workshop?

37 Stand on the line—scattergram

JEFF KINDER

Description

A way to engage participants' physical 'knowing' and put it in tune with their intellectual understanding of their present level of knowledge about a topic.

TIME **15 min.**
Approximately 15 minutes, depending on the size of the group.

Learning opportunity

• To allow participants in a conference, workshop or learning program to get to know one another and at the same time appreciate that all participants come to the course with different backgrounds and levels of experience and self-confidence.

GROUP SIZE 3–15
3–15 people.

Audience

This exercise can be used early on the first day of longer programs. It assists participants to build rapport with one another and can promote team building through the physical process of gaining insight into similarities and differences.

Resources

You'll need:

• 1 long ribbon (at least 3 m) stretched along the floor, or a similar strip of masking tape stuck to the floor or a chalk line drawn on the floor
• 2 signs, one titled *Complete novice (no experience)* and the other titled *Complete expert (exhaustive experience)*—one placed at one end of the line, the other at the other end of the line (examples supplied)
• A second ribbon or tape (approximately equal in length to the first) to be placed on the floor, part way through the activity
• 2 more signs, one titled *High level of comfort (self-confidence)* and another titled *Low level of comfort (self-confidence)* (examples supplied)

Setting

Any room or outdoor area with a flat floor and sufficient space to allow people to move about freely.

Briefing

- Announce that the line of ribbon or tape represents the degree to which people are either *Complete novices* (point to the notice, representing this position, at one end of the line) or *Complete experts* (point to the notice at the other end of the line).
- Add that a second line representing *Level of comfort* will be positioned later.

Process

- Ask participants to 'stand on the line at the spot which best represents your current level of experience in *the skill being trained*'.
- Once everyone begins to move, join the line yourself at the point which represents your own 'capability level' with the content you will be teaching.
- Place the second ribbon (or tape) on the floor at a right angle to the first line and half way down its length. Stretch it out and secure it to the floor.
- Place the remaining signs on the new line (as per the diagram).
- Ask all participants to think quietly for a moment and, when ready, move into the matrix according to their level of confidence (i.e. if they feel quite confident, they move towards the sign; if they are not yet comfortable they may move further away from it).
- They must hold their position relative to the spot they chose on the first line. Thus everyone will move into 1 of the 4 quartiles formed by the 2 tapes.
- This will result in a *scattergram* of people in a variety of positions representing both their level of knowledge and their level of confidence in using it, and lead directly into the debriefing (with people still standing in their chosen positions).

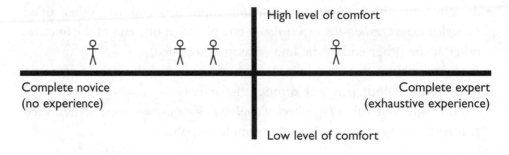

High level of comfort

Complete novice
(no experience)

Complete expert
(exhaustive experience)

Low level of comfort

Debriefing

Keep the pace moving along and light-hearted, allowing time for all people to participate.
  Ask:

- What are your reasons for attending this course?
- What do you hope to gain from your attendance?
- What things did you learn about others in the group?
- Do you feel more like a member of a team now?
- Did anyone feel threatened or uneasy at all about the exercise? What made it so?
- How did this exercise represent what happens when a team first comes together?
- People chose to stand in different places on the line. Why do you think this happened? Possible influencing factors could include:
  - past experiences
  - prior learning, education, training
  - personal attitude, tensions
  - perceptions and individual learning styles (auditory, visual and/or kinaesthetic—sense of touch—emotional responsiveness)
  - the country and culture of our formative years
  - our upbringing, needs and desires
  - our family, friends and their options
  - religion, morals and values
  - even the influence of the press and media
- Comment that the trainer(s) will also be learning and improving. We can all learn from each other. You may want to link learners with significant experience to those who are beginners, and build a support network to bring beginners up to speed and help to overcome some of the difficulties when members of a group have a diverse range of prior knowledge.
- To revise the progress of learners' levels of self-confidence and experience, the matrix can be revisited during or after a learning program to monitor learners' perceptions and to develop their awareness of the extent to which course objectives are being achieved.

Complete novice
(no experience)

Complete expert
(exhaustive experience)

High level of comfort
(self-confidence)

Low level of comfort (self-confidence)

38 Coloured shapes

SANDRA CHUNG

TIME   **1 hour**

Approximately 60 minutes (depending on the number of groups):
- 15 minutes for preparation
- 5–7 minutes for each presentation
- 10 minutes for debriefing

GROUP SIZE   **30**

Up to approximately 30 people (e.g. 5 subgroups, each of 6 people).

Description

A fun game using the concept of a jigsaw to link participants in small groups.

Learning opportunity

- To change group dynamics by bringing participants into teams that differ from any groupings that may already exist.
- To energise a group and have fun.
- To encourage participants to discuss topics and/or statements, perhaps for revision.
- To help teams to pool their knowledge and present ideas to a larger group.

Audience

Any trainees at any time during training.

Resources

You'll need:

- Different coloured sheets of thick paper or cardboard that have been cut into interesting shapes (e.g. clouds, stars, triangles or parallelograms) with 1 topic heading boldly written on each shape so that the writing covers much of the shape. For example, if you have 5 shapes and 20 participants, cut each shape into 4 pieces: 5 x 4 = 20. The 4 topic headings can be chosen from anything relevant to what is being trained
- 1 envelope for each participant

Setting

Enough room for people to move around, form teams, discuss and present.

Briefing

Place 1 piece of coloured board or paper into each envelope and distribute them to participants. If this is done before a session starts, it will make group members curious about what is going to happen with these coloured shapes.

Process

- Ask participants to open their envelope and then to find the other pieces to put together a coloured shape (e.g. a cloud, star, triangle or parallelogram).
- Participants are to form discussion teams and prepare a mini-presentation on the relevant topic that has been revealed through putting together the shape. Their mini-presentation is to be fed back to the whole group. Allow 15 minutes for preparation and 5–7 minutes for each presentation.

Debriefing

After the presentations, use the remaining 10 minutes to ask participants:

- How did members feel when they matched their pieces into coloured shapes?
- Did members find that others had similar, or opposing, ideas on the topic or how to present it?
- As a facilitator, reflect on how this activity changed usual group-forming patterns and how the game can be used to prepare members for the next part of the training.

Sample templates (1)

(Your key words are written in large letters inside each shape.)

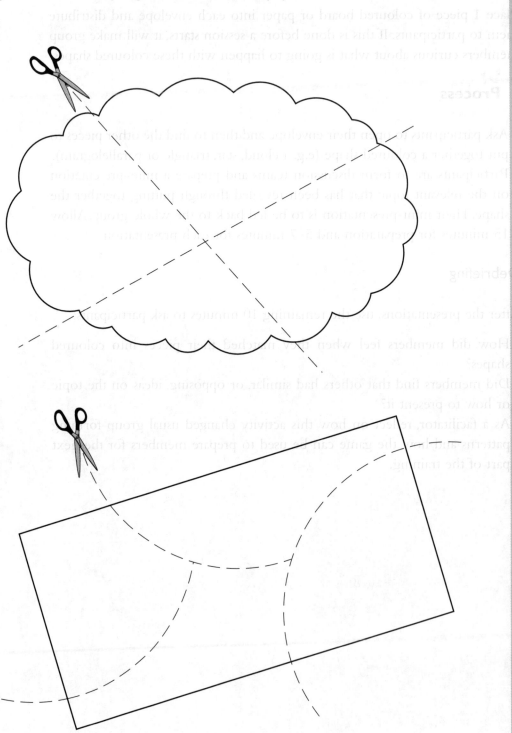

Sample templates (2)

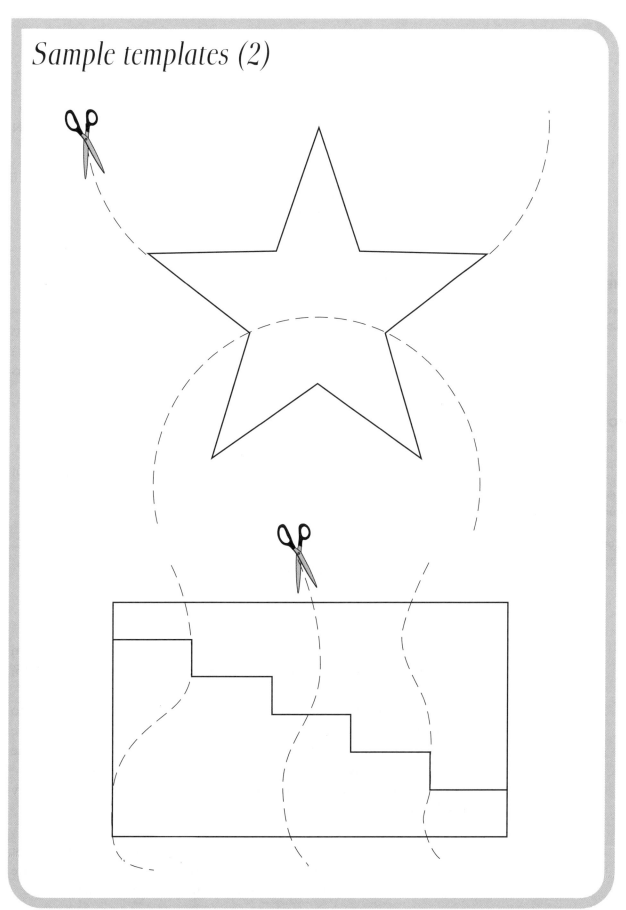

39

CARP (clarify and reinforce points)

JUDITH WILLIAMSON

TIME 15–20 min.

Approximately 15–20 minutes.

Description

A game based on sorting cards into matched sets. The text on each card is created by the facilitator beforehand and arranged so that there are multiple sets of 3 matching cards. The content of each card helps review knowledge introduced in a learning program, and promotes discussion and debate as players compete to get the most sets of matched cards.

GROUP SIZE 5+

Any number of small groups with 2–5 people per group. This game can even be used in solitude as a matching review activity for one person revising alone.

Learning opportunity

• To review important points from a training session and to identify areas that may still require clarification.

Audience

Any learners who can benefit from clarification and reinforcement.

Resources

• You'll need sets of blank playing card size cards. You can cut paper to form a pack of at least 12 cards, but preferable more, in multiples of 3 (i.e. 12, 15, 18, 21, etc.).
• Review and identify a number of key issues that you'd like participants to review. Write a word, phrase or short sentence that denotes each issue to be reviewed on separate cards (e.g. networking with people). These form the first cards in matched sets of 3 (see sample sets below for examples).
• Next, repeat the idea or concept, using a different phrase or a closely matched or associated idea on a second card.
• Write a third card to complete a match.
• Continue the process for as many sets as you plan to use. Complete at least 4 matched sets (for a minimum of 12 cards) to form a pack of cards. Prepare a separate pack of the same cards for each group you plan to have.

• Sample sets of cards:

Networking with people	Answer by the third ring
Making contacts	Give a polite greeting
Building relationships	Use the caller's name regularly

Setting

Tables (or other flat surfaces, e.g. floor space) large enough to spread the cards out so that none are overlapping, and so that players also have space in front of them to lay out sets of cards they have matched.

Briefing

• Explain that the activity is intended to help review the information presented in the training session.
• Use 1 pack of cards to demonstrate the process and explain the rules.
• If you want to make it competitive, say that the winner is the person with the most completed sets of cards at the end of the game.

Process

• Arrange participants in small groups of 2–5 people.
• Pass out a pack of cards to each group.
• Participants shuffle cards and spread them out, face down, so that none overlap.
• The first player turns over any 3 cards, keeping them in their place on the table. If the cards don't make a matched set, they are turned back face down.

If they do form a matched set, the player explains how and why they are linked (to clarify and reinforce the learning). The matched cards are then moved and displayed in front of the player, who takes another turn.

- If the player does not turn over a matched set or cannot see the connection, the cards are turned down again and the next player tries to find a matched set by turning over any 3 cards.
- Cards are turned down again even if 2 of the 3 match.
- Play continues until all cards have been matched.
- No player is to tell or indicate to others the location of matching cards during the game.
- Players can agree or disagree as to whether or not the 3 cards selected by a player do match. In all cases, the player must give a sound rationale about the connection among all 3 cards.
- The winner is the person with the most sets of matched cards after all sets have been matched.

Debriefing

Review all the matched cards with the whole group to ensure there has been consistency in their understanding and then ask participants:

- What happened?
- How did you feel as you played the game?
- What information did you find easy to match?
- Which areas did you find difficult?
- What were the stumbling blocks?
- How did you overcome barriers?
- What did you learn from this activity?
- What discussions took place?

40 Exploring ethical dilemmas

ELYSSEBETH LEIGH

Description

A two part exploration of issues arising from the experience of real-life events. Participants work in small groups to explore real ethical dilemmas through a sequence of description, discussion, exploration and analysis.

Learning opportunity

This activity enables individuals to learn more about their own ethical positions and personal values through a process of describing an actual problem they face (or have faced) and then accepting commentary and analysis from others before giving their opinions of others' problems and values positions. It does not encourage people to judge each other or develop 'shared values'.

Audience

Any group of adults who are exploring their own values and ethics in workplace contexts.

Resources

You'll need:

- Sheets of blank paper—about 5 per participant
- Pens or pencils (preferably black or another very dark colour for ease of copying)
- A photocopier close by (to make duplicates of each participant's 'ethical dilemma')
- Seats for everyone

Setting

Any flat area where small groups of 4 or 5 people can sit together without being disturbed by other groups.

TIME 1.5 hours

A minimum of 60 minutes for the first session and 30 minutes for the second session. More time may be needed if the dilemmas posed are complex and require in-depth analysis.

GROUP SIZE 8–24

This activity can be played by groups of up to about 24, as long as it is possible to create small groups each of 4 (or 5) members per group.

213

Briefing

- Introduce the activity by suggesting that we all frequently face dilemmas which involve making decisions based on what we hold to be 'true', 'valid', 'important', 'honourable' or 'ethical'.
- Ask everyone to bring to mind (but not to speak about) such a situation that has happened to them recently. It does not need to be a major dramatic dilemma: in fact, smaller ones are easier to explore and can be used to open up discussion of what is important to us.
- Explain that this involves them writing a brief description of the situation and sharing it with 3 or 4 other people—but no more than that.
- Tell them that you will be keeping track of time and moving them through a series of action steps; their task will be to focus on the problems and issues that arise, while you take care of the logistics and timekeeping.

Process

Session I

- Arrange participants into groups of 4 (or 5) and explain that they will be working together.
- Distribute blank sheets of paper and black pens and announce that they have 5 minutes to write a brief description of a particular incident, or a general problem, concerning their own sense of ethics and values that they are encountering, and feel able to share with others.
- Allow 5 minutes for writing about their problem.
- At the end of 5 minutes collect the pages, keeping each set of 4 (or 5) papers together.
- Make 3 (or 4, if using groups of 5) copies of each set of papers.
- While the copying is being done, ask the groups to discuss their answers to the question: *What is an ethical position?* They are required to write a definition. The purpose is to open up their thinking and encourage them to consider the problematic nature of what is being discussed. It is not about getting answers.
- Distribute the sets of sheets so that each participant has copies of all the stories written by all the members of their set.
- Allow 5–10 minutes for reading. Ensure there is silence and enough time to reflect about what they have read.
- Announce that set members must agree on the order in which they will discuss their stories and that each person will have the same amount of time to explain, discuss and gather ideas and comments about their story. You will

be timekeeping and the discussion sequence must be strictly timed. You will announce each change of action as follows:
  – 2 minutes to explain (this enables them to explain more about what they wrote, since we do think about things differently once we see them objectively and know that others are also reading them);
  – 5 minutes for questions of clarification from the storyteller;
  – 2–3 minutes for silent reflection and writing by everyone about what has been suggested and any other (often unrelated) ideas that come to mind;
  – 5 minutes for the group to suggest options for action on the story. The suggestions must be for action, not just sympathy or exploration. The storyteller listens and seeks clarification but does not say: 'That will not work where I am.' This is a form of non-written brainstorming. Emphasise that we can reject ideas so fast that we don't even realise that we have heard them, let alone considered them.

• The storyteller then responds to the suggestions by saying 'I think that…because…' about each suggestion, and/or suggests an order of priority in which they could apply the ideas.

• They undertake to spend some time during the coming week applying one action or observing the simulation and deciding whether any of the suggestions would work if the problem (as described) arises again.

• Once this sequence is completed for the first storyteller, the next one begins and the timekeeping is repeated until everyone has told their story and received feedback.

• Finally, when everyone has had their turn, remind them that their reflections are to be reported to the same set at the beginning of the next session together. What they will be reporting on is their reflections and observations and not necessarily the results of any actions; the emphasis is on the quality and attention to reflection.

Session 2

• During the next session with the group, set aside at least 30 minutes for each set to review what they discussed in the first session, what has happened since then, and what they are now thinking about in regard to their general position on ethics and values at work.

Debriefing

Once everyone has completed the second session you may wish to conduct a general discussion about how the process helped individuals learn more about ethics and values at work. Useful questions include:

- What is different about your understanding of ethics and values as a result of this process?
- What particular issues were most difficult to explore?
- Why were they difficult?
- Did anyone find themselves changing their position on particular issues?
- What factors were influencing them?
- Did the process help people to clarify their own ethical position and values? How did it do this?
- What problems remain unresolved at this time?